PRAISE FOR TH

Using journals and recordings made while Nancy and her husband David faced the end of his life, Nancy Klein Maguire makes sense of love, intimacy, and death. *The Monk's Widow* shows marriage partners facing the finitude of life, and, ultimately, finding their own brave form of transcendence.
  Michael Witmore, Director, Folger Shakespeare Library

The singularity, honesty, and vulnerability of *The Monk's Widow* creates an authenticity that speaks for itself. It can't be faked. It's either real and true, or it isn't. And so, through its intimate truth-telling, the reach of *The Monk's Widow* is deep and wide, bordering on universal. This is beautiful.
  Dr. Joan Gibson, bioethicist

The Monk's Widow is a beautifully written and moving account of a shared journey through the borderland of the undiscovered country. It should be read by all those who must confront the process of dying, whether as family members, caregivers, or medical professionals.
    Dr. Lee F. Elliott, physician

The Monk's Widow is a very powerful book. Thank you for letting me read it. David told you "Do something that can't be done – then you have a chance of getting it right." You have certainly done that, at least twice. First with helping David die, and second with this book.
    Amanda Helman Gordon, author

Told from a voice filled with vulnerable strength, *The Monk's Widow* demonstrates that love stories do not need to fit into a perfect mold in order to be profound and true.
    Rev. Jana Troutman Miller, chaplain

Nancy Klein Maguire sheds light on the acts of death, dying, medical confusion and eventually loneliness. With our aging population growing, more and more people will face these problems, but Maguire's narrative will help them navigate a complex and emotional journey.

    Gene Croisant, senior corporate executive and consultant

I sat down to read a few chapters of *The Monk's Widow* and couldn't stop. I read all the way through. Your writing is as clear as a bell. The introduction particularly had me hooked - not because it's about death, but because it's about life and its most sacred partnership, marriage. As a young person who just got married, I can tell you that death isn't on my mind (yet). But marriage is a total enigma - only the two people who are "in it" can understand the depths and layers that compound over the years.

    Emily Miller, entrepreneur

You did a really good job of capturing time and what I perceived as a painfully slow slog of dealing with uncharted territory. You captured it so well that I was having a physical reaction while reading it. Definitely not an easy read, but I couldn't stop reading it. Thanks for sharing it.
    Daniel Baumstark, physical therapist

The Monk's Widow is so honest, so painful, and yet so positive that I have experienced the difficulties of your immense pain and joy at David's prolonged passing. Congratulations on an extremely thought-provoking and medically correct masterpiece.
    Alan Goldberg, MD PhD

When I read *The Monk's Widow*, I was amazed that Maguire is able to articulate her authentic feelings during the twenty-six months of David's dying. When I consider my husband's illness and death, I am able to give a generalized statement of my feelings, but not the specific authentic feelings. Nancy's relationship to David was so concentrated that there was no room for attention to any other subject.
    Beatrice Belda Pronley, widow

Copyright © 2022 by Nancy Klein Maguire

All rights reserved. No part of this publication may be reproduced, distributed or transmitted in any form or by any means, including photocopying, recording, digital scanning or other electronic or mechanical methods, without prior written permission of the copyright owner except for the use of quotations in a book review.

For permission requests:
contact@nancykleinmaguire.com
Published 2022
Printed in the United States of America

Print ISBN: 979-8-9857615-0-4
E-ISBN: 979-8-9857615-2-8
Library of Congress Control Number: 2022906774
For information, address: The Solitary Press, 500 Trinity Lane, Suite 3111, St. Petersburg Florida. 33716-1224

Book design by Moon Design
Cover Painting by Laura Loe

All company and/or product names may be trade names, logos, trademarks and/or registered trademarks and are the property of their respective owners.
www.nancykleinmaguire.com

The Monk's Widow

A Memoir of a Resilient Love and Intimate Death

NANCY KLEIN MAGUIRE

AUTHOR NOTES

This book is a memoir, actually, a double memoir. *The Monk's Widow* is our story, my story, my understanding of our fifty-year relationship, seven years after David's death. My goal has been to document the raw human emotions accompanying the death of a spouse, particularly the emotions of a caregiver spouse. The people who knew us, especially during the twenty-six months of David's dying time, may have a different and completely authentic story

Douglas Evans, MD, the head of the cancer center and a kind and trusted physician, has given me permission to use his name in this book. I have not identified the other numerous physicians in the story by name, rather by function. If I needed a name to help the reader, I invented a first name. I also created first names for two people I've not been able to locate. Everyone else, but one, has allowed me to use their first names.

David's job was to die, my job was to write this book, a difficult job. I needed to relive those twenty-six months; reliving them, frankly, has been more difficult than living them. I did this job 24/7 for five years. I live part time in Washington D.C., a half mile from the Folger Shakespeare Library, where I have spent my professional life. My other life remains at our home in the Allegheny Mountains.

Honoring Courageous Caretaker Spouses,
with compassion and respect.

I take you, to have and to hold, for better or worse, in sickness and in health,
until death do us part.
Catholic wedding vow

When David had finished speaking to Saul, the soul of Jonathan was bound to
the soul of David.
1 Samuel 18:1

If it be not to come, it will be now; If it be not now, it will come.
The readiness is all.
Hamlet, 5:2 William Shakespeare

"Writing keeps you focused and compelling in your presentation. Stick with the truth. No matter what may come at you. It is on your tombstone and it has always been the driver of your scholarship and personal life. You stood by your guns in this deal and it all came to you."

David E. Maguire, April 8, 2015

PREFACE

Long marriages can be complicated. David and I had many marriages, probably twelve, all of them powerful relationships. We had some marriages off-the-charts good, so good that we hoped they were permanent. We also had pretty terrible years. Any marriage counselor would have suggested we not get married in the first place, or get divorced. Looking at our marriage through the lens of David's lethal liver cancer, I am amazed that we stuck it out for forty-eight years. We were radically different in every way, with no plans to change.

Our goals were diametrically opposed, and we consciously blocked each other from achieving them. As a young Carthusian monk, David had lived by his will and intellect. He wanted to retain this identity: monastic reserve, detachment, privacy, and lack of emotion. I wanted intimacy. When at age twenty-three, I extricated myself, after seven years, from a Catholic convent, I had one goal: to know as many people as possible, as deeply as possible. This worked well for me until I met David. Intimacy is not part of monkish-ness, and, besides, David was ambivalent about being married.

I thought we would never stop sparring, arguing over the

meaning of life, as well as everything else. While we could not live without each other, we proved over and over that we could not live with each other. We desperately looked for an angle of repose, and found it only in living apart. David's rare and lethal cancer, and our decision not to seek further treatment, gave us our last chance to resolve our relationship.

Death coerced us, compelled us, to come to terms with our ambivalent and challenging marriage. We decided to work together, to make something good come from this cancer. We turned our death into a project. During our regular evening conversations, David checked to make sure we stayed on the same dying page. I took fieldnotes, often on scraps of paper, collected letters, and medical documentation. Most critically, we recorded our evening conversations on my iPhone. I do not believe there is another record quite like this.

These sixty-some recordings are perhaps the closest anyone can get to witnessing the unfiltered experience of dying with a terminal illness. They provided a skeleton for this book, authenticating my account of David's dying in precise detail. They gave me something I have not had in my other work – tone of voice, timber, level of exhaustion, anxiety, deep grief, and, at times, terror. We both steadily watched his slow disintegration, witnessed his impossibly slow death. I recorded it.

The record of this very slow and complicated walk to the end is unique, answering questions not yet considered. How does the decision to die deliberately and consciously live out? How do you feel? What do you think about? What do you need? How do you control your panic, depression? How do you tolerate the wait? I was my most scholarly self, my most authentic self, during this time. After this death, everything else seemed insignificant, and not worth pursuing. The dying experience was sacred. Being a wife/caregiver/ethnographer was difficult, but looking back, I would not have missed our ending:

complete acceptance and respect, along with a measure of peace.

I did not choose to write *The Monk's Widow*. I had to write the book for myself, for David, for our relationship. To survive, to reclaim my identity, to reconstruct myself, I needed to write this memoir. When I stumbled out of the funeral time in the long weeks and months of widowhood, I had the sense that so much had happened I could never put it together. I couldn't stop trying to capture this ultimate human experience. I needed to understand the mystery of our death, what had happened to our team. I couldn't find the words to say it. There were always too many words; I needed to become a poet.

Not until two years later would words start to come, but each word had a bloody birth. And then the words came so fast, like a torrent rushing out of the river, that I couldn't contain them, and they just flowed onto my computer. Everything wanted to be said at once. I tried to find a way to control the words; I created chapters and then more chapters. Eventually, after twenty months of flashbacks, of reliving/writing our death, I could stop for a bit. Complete rough draft finished.

During the early pandemic, living alone, I revised endlessly. The virtual, but constant, presence of the covid deaths, especially the presence of the widowed caregivers, kept me reliving, revising, in hope that *The Monk's Widow* might help covid victims.

1

SPARRING PARTNERS

Rejoice. On May 18, 2015, David Edward Maguire died in Milwaukee, Wisconsin. Born March 2, 1938, Maguire was a graduate of St. Mary of the Lake Seminary, St. Hugh's Charterhouse, Sussex, England, and the University of Chicago. He was most fortunate to live and work with exceptional and caring people, most notably, his spouse and sparring partner of 48 years, Dr. Nancy Klein Maguire.

My relationship with David Maguire was very intense, and there was a lot of ambivalence. When we were together, we argued continually, challenging each other, each of us trying to control every situation. We often said, "We never should've got married." My question was: should we have stayed married. But, we did. We seemed unable to separate. Besides, we were always much too busy to take the time for a divorce.

So, there we were. Two years before he died, David wrote his obituary in which he referred to me as his "spouse and sparring partner." He thought I would object, but the phrase seemed to be absolutely true, although not what one would expect in an obituary. Most of the time, we enjoyed sparring, keeping ourselves alert by invariably challenging each other. David absolutely needed to be in control, and I absolutely needed not to be controlled. He would tell me to do something, and usually I just wouldn't do it. Then I would complain that he was always telling me what to do. A friend at dinner commented, "but you never do what he tells you to do, so what difference does it make?" When we did our shtick in an ER, the doctor commented, "people would pay to see this."

David and I argued almost by habit. It really never stopped until the very end. On the surface, the arguments were always over one thing: who was in control, who was in charge. We both thought we were the boss, and we tenaciously held a position. We were very competitive and fiercely guarded our turf. Numbers, for example, were David's turf, words were mine. When David started doing the Saturday *New York Times* crossword puzzle, he knew words that I didn't know. I was jealous and upset.

On a deeper level, the battle was over God, the purpose of life. We both were monotheists, but he really believed in a personal God, while I believed in a Creator who may or may not be interested in the creatures. We were both God seekers, but David expected to see God in the next life, and I looked for him/her in this life. I didn't even use the word "God," I would use the word "transcendence." We were both looking for a spiritual reality; during the last months, and even weeks, of David's life, we talked about this sort of thing. David always objected to "transcendence;" he would say, "That is your word, not mine." Whatever the word, we both struggled to find it. He respected my dedication to the humanities. I did my best to respect his monastic searching.

As David and I went through the twenty-six months from prognosis to death, we had some of the most violent of our sparring events. They were simply damn fights, vile fights. The battle raged until the very end. We argued a lot during our first forty-six years, but nothing ever approached the intensity of our fight over David's death. In facing cholangiocarcinoma, bile duct cancer, we did the usual thing; we argued about it. We were off the charts bad, our relationship would have been the worst example of emotional abuse, on both sides, of any marriage in the divorce courts.

I thought we would have to hire a marriage counselor so that David could die in peace. In fact, we did. A social worker tried to help us figure out the best use of the time we had. Our ideas about how to use this time, of course, differed vastly. We both wanted to do this death right, but we had different beliefs about what was right.

David did not want to die; he did not want to leave me, but when faced with certain death, he jumped right back into the time slot of a Carthusian monk who "wanted to see the face of the living God," a Carthusian phrase, but certainly Old Testament. And now, half a century later, he saw his chance. "Nancy, get out of my way. Nancy, rejoice with me that I'm going to get to God. I want to run a good race." In the worst of this fight, he said, "You are an albatross hanging around my neck. You are supposed to rejoice." I countered with, "we should be mourning the loss of our life, the loss of our home, the loss of us." I had never been this angry in my entire life – he was forbidding me to mourn. I'm emotional, passionately emotional, and he was trying to eradicate my identity.

Rage, rage, rage against the dying of David. "Are you out of your mind? Don't you think I will miss you?" This vile fight went on for over an hour, in front of three aghast spectators. One commented, "there is enough energy in this room to fuel the entire building;" another tried to help me out, "David, you don't have to rub her face in it," the third, a Jewish woman, looking dazed, said, "you two are not from different cultures, you are from different galaxies." They were right. We put a tremendous amount of energy in this, our most fundamental fight. We were not only arguing about who was in control, we were arguing about our fundamental approach to the meaning of life. When the spectators left, David wandered off to our bedroom and went to bed. Soon after, I walked into our bedroom and slammed my iPad onto the nightstand. David jumped up out of bed and said, "I thought you were going to shoot me." He pretended he didn't care that I was so angry, but it really upset him.

After several weeks, and even months, we finally resolved this fight in a negotiated treaty; David agreed to tolerate my tears, and I agreed to respect, and promised not to trivialize, monkhood. The monks were always my biggest enemy. Like nearly every ex-monk that I've known, David couldn't stop wanting to go back to the Charterhouse, a Carthusian monastery. Even after we were married, he would think about going back to the Charterhouse, he preferred God to me. Intolerable. Why then did he marry me? I asked this over and over again for forty-eight years. He said, at least twice a month, "I never for a minute regretted marrying you." Why? He often responded, "I knew I would never be bored, and I wasn't." I never said I never regretted marrying him, but I wasn't bored either.

Even though our cultural backgrounds appeared to be similar, at heart they were very different. David was an only child of elderly parents who been told they could not have a child. His mother thought he was, at least, Jesus Christ, and David was a good example of Freud's dictum, "whoever is the mother's favorite child will always feel like a conqueror." David had an uncanny, and devastating, skill to make people do what he wanted them to do, while they thought it was what they wanted to do. Everyone liked David, even though he was always the best at everything – which is not as hard as it seems if you never do anything in which you are not the best.

David went to college in a major seminary in Mundelein, Illinois, which was like a country club, with its own golf course and private lake. He studied philosophy and theology until he was twenty-three. After being first in class in every subject, he joined the Carthusians, an order of hermit monks. It was his choice. He cherished the solo life; he lived in his own cell, actually a 1500-square-foot, three-story building in Horsham, England. After nearly five years of solitude, he left and returned to his home in Chicago, Illinois. He did not have a plan, not a clue, as to what he would do next, but he was ecstatic as he walked away from the Charterhouse.

David loved every minute of his religious experience. I hated every minute of mine, due to the huge gender disparity in the Catholic Church. My mother, with the encouragement of two of her religious siblings, a priest and a nun, enrolled me in a convent, actually a rather brutal one, much like the movie *The Magdalene Sisters*. I cleaned toilets, laundered sanitary napkins, washed dishes, waited on table, made coifs, and taught forty-seven third and fourth graders. I was trained to be one more cog in the convent conveyor belt; my brain shut down by excellent brainwashing. I expected to stay for a few months, but I wasn't able to escape for seven brutalizing years.

Before I made final vows, obliging me to stay there forever, my twenty-three-year-old brain thought its way out of mindless obedience. I got out, but I brought a lot of baggage with me. For nearly four decades, I woke in cold sweats, usually three times a week, with the same nightmare: I'm in the convent and cannot get out. Every convent night, I had gone to bed hoping I would not wake up. Waking up was like facing a jail sentence for life.

Recovering from that jail sentence was a challenge. Fighting hard to find my post-convent life, I earned, in just four years, a BA and MA at Marquette University in Milwaukee, Wisconsin. While there, I fell passionately in love, smoked, organized seven parties in seven days, and was known locally as the Pearl Mesta, the socialite, of Marquette.

Two years later, I was teaching literature in the English department at Loyola University in downtown Chicago. I loved university teaching, and I loved being in downtown Chicago, right in the middle of everything. Finally, a very happy spinster —I had my own Murphy bed apartment (with a sewer gas leak), a red Corvair, an electric typewriter, and the best stereo that could be had in Chicago. At last, my life was exactly the way I wanted it. I was safe and happy in my world. Until …

On January 19, 1967, seven days before the big snow storm, Rita, the only other woman on the English faculty, came up to me and said, "My nephew Chuck, an ex-monk, asked me to help a friend, another ex-monk." Then, she asked, "Would you have a cup of coffee with us at Charmays on Chicago Avenue?" Did I have to? Yet one more ex-seminarian? I had just finished a twelve-hour teaching day, wearing three-inch heels with pointy toes. My feet ached and all I wanted to do was to soak them in a tub of hot water. But, I reluctantly agreed. When I opened the door to my basement office at 9 p.m., Rita appeared and said, "This is David. Have fun, you two." How did this turn into my first blind date? What is wrong with Rita who was single? I thought I'd made it clear that I liked being single.

I was David's ninth date; the other ones were either too eager or not interested, but this one hit a high note from the start. He took me to a French restaurant, Coq au Vin, on the near North Side. On my teacher's salary, I did not even know restaurants like Coq Au Vin existed. His suit seemed a bit shabby, but he certainly knew how to order in an expensive French restaurant. For a monk, he knew his way around. After we made our selections, he confidently ordered for me: "The lady will have." I liked his old-fashioned manner, his confidence, his ease in the secular environment, his ability to live in the world.

We had barely started dinner when he opened his wallet and showed me his passport picture—an intense monk with no hair. I was interested. He had been something I couldn't be, a contemplative. I had thought I was much too gregarious for a contemplative life, but it was the life I had wanted since I read Thomas Merton's *The Seven-Story Mountain* when I was sixteen, even when I was in a non-contemplative convent. David was confident of himself, sure of himself, I have never been sure of myself. He could look me in the eye without blinking, without any defenses or safeguards—no one else had ever been able to do that. Not blinking suggested complete trust and openness. He could not do it again until the last few weeks of his life.

David had thrived on the solitude and brainwork of the monastery, and, after a few years, he clearly was the best at singing. He soon was responsible for teaching the young monks how to sing. But, after many months, they were still always off pitch. He had failed when had not failed before. In his words, "I could live with the off-pitch monks, I couldn't live with not doing a good job." David always had done everything exceptionally well, could not live with not doing a competent job. After nearly five years, David left the Carthusian monastery.

While David told me he left because he couldn't keep the monks on pitch. I suspect his decision to leave was more than his failure to keep the monks on pitch. It was essential to him to do the job well. Even though, he was shooting under par when he was sixteen, he gave up golf because he recognized that the younger people would be better than he was. Perhaps he wasn't sure he would be an outstanding monk. Perhaps too many of his talents were underutilized. Whatever his motive, he was jubilant when he left. When we met his novice master at the Charterhouse in 1999, the novice master said: "it is good that you left because you have so much more to contribute on the outside."

Since he was no longer a monk, he thought he should get married. He needed an identity, a place within the purview of the Catholic Church; being a bachelor was not a vocation like being a monk. David always got what he wanted, and after shopping around, he decided he wanted me. I had something he didn't have—emotion. David actually had many emotions, but he didn't identify them or experience them consciously, or even have any awareness of them. He never even knew what emotion he was experiencing. Rarely expressed, his anger usually flared when someone had injured me or not properly recognized me. As a child, David had learned to totally block his fears and anxieties with his considerable intelligence and willpower; his impenetrable armor protected him from any emotional assault.

David rigorously encased himself in a barrier of kryptonite. He was extraordinarily reserved, and no one knew what he was thinking. He had no experience of intimate relationships, told me little of himself, except his monk life and playing golf. The first personal thing he told me, and told me frequently, was an experience when he was three years old. His parents had told him that they all were going on a road trip to a golf resort, but, they dumped him with a stranger in Florida. He never forgot and made sure he was never left behind again. He didn't tell me much else until much later. I suspect he didn't remember his early life, at least he didn't talk about it until the last decade or so of our marriage.

Reserved or not, David pursued me with determination: flowers on every week anniversary of January 19, dinner at every expensive restaurant in Chicago, and walks around the city. Our first real date was a movie on Chicago Avenue: *A Man and a Woman*, a 1966 French film. I had been very interested in movies, especially foreign movies, and thought it was technically a great movie. David thought it was a great relationship; perhaps he was looking for a great love, equal to his love of God.

During the big snow of 1967, we took an L to Evanston, a Chicago suburb, to see *Doctor Zhivago*. The "Laura" song stayed with us to the end. David knew Chicago very well, and when the city was totally snowed in, he walked us through tunnels to the Wrigley Building bridge. The city was totally empty, except for the two of us on the bridge. In my business school poetry course, the men studied love poetry for the entire semester. They all stood up and cheered *Brava* when I finally walked in with an engagement ring. Thank God, the end of love poetry.

On one of our walks, we met some of his priest friends coming out of an Italian restaurant on Wells Street, and he did not even introduce me. He still thought he was a monk, I guess. I should've been worried at this point. One evening a few weeks later, when we were in my apartment, he started talking about how he might want to go back to the monastery. I started crying hysterically, cried for four hours. I had believed this relationship was real, not make-believe. I had trusted him, and now, he was talking of leaving me forever, going back to a weird monastery? This seemed to envelop all of the abandonment I had ever experienced.

I don't think David had ever seen a woman cry; he himself never cried a single tear in his entire life. He did not want to leave me while I was crying, but unmarried Catholic couples did not stay overnight in each other's apartments, so he left about midnight. At 6 a.m., he came back and told me he had decided I was more important than the monastery. Anything to stop me from crying.

I wanted David, but I didn't necessarily want to be married. I was ambivalent. I thoroughly enjoyed my independence as a single person. I really liked being single; after my stint in a convent, independence was critical to me. After about five weeks, David proposed and gave me an ultimatum: make up your mind by Mother's Day, or I will look elsewhere.

My immediate response was: "No one gives me an ultimatum." But, we went through the meeting of the family thing, having dinner with his parents in a downtown restaurant; they seemed very proper, very reserved, and a bit older than my parents. David was uncomfortable introducing his parents to me. Clearly, I was not the North Shore debutante David's mother had wanted. David met my mother and the available siblings in Milwaukee where my brother Peter was in the seminary. My dad had died four years earlier, so we went to Mader's, Dad's favorite German restaurant. My siblings were curious and not particularly friendly, but my mother was ecstatic that I finally might get married. David was overwhelmed by my family, but he wrote a gracious note to my mother, praising the diversity and independence of her children.

Until later, I did not tell David that I had been in the convent. I had worked for seven years to block out that shameful experience, I kept this information from everyone. Even though I did not tell him until we were practically engaged, there was some sense of familiarity, of hope that he could understand me, and hope that I could understand him. We didn't need to talk when we were together, I didn't have to be a live wire or entertaining; we were content just to be together. We both needed space. It seemed right. I felt we were like Jonathan and David in the Old Testament. I loved David like I had loved God, with the love of my lost saints. That description always seemed true, but David never understood it.

At our wedding dinner, David's toast was: "For Nancy, who put a song in my heart, a spring to my step, and meaning to my life." We left the wedding reception early, at David's insistence; the next day, we left for our honeymoon in Scotland, Wales, and England. We fought so much I was amazed we didn't get divorced before we returned home. Our trip to David's monastery was a disaster. As we walked the long path to the monastery, a Carthusian brother met us, saying, "Dom Philip, I knew you would come back." Four days after the wedding! The prior, Dom Guy, met us in a really uncomfortable and dark parlor and refused to let me see the inside of the monastery. David walked me around the exterior so I could see over the wall. The cells were actually three-story houses. Enough of monks.

Our biggest battle was over Shakespeare. On the day of Jason Robards' performance in *Macbeth* at Stratford upon Avon, fifty standing room only tickets were reserved. I went to stand in line at six in the morning, while David had a leisurely breakfast at our B&B, chatting it up with a child actor in the play. David showed up at ten as the ticket person was offering me either a ticket in the front row or standing room. Before I could say anything, David butted in and said, "standing room." I was eager to get home to get divorced. We were just beginning to learn our highly refined art of sparring.

After surviving the honeymoon, we had a fairly ordinary early marriage, except that I was David's first roommate, as well as the first woman he kissed. David seemed to contain all of virility. I would look down on Sheridan Road from our apartment on the thirteenth floor, and see David coming home from work wearing a felt grown-up hat and a long grown-up jacket. I thought he was so beautiful. To his outrage, I once called him Beauty.

Before we were engaged, David had warned me that he did not do domestic labor, monks just prayed. He did his best to continue living like a monk—it took me weeks to convince him to take a shower every week. He had never tried to cook, never done his own laundry, never cleaned the kitchen, or bought his own clothes, and he was not eager to begin. After I left the convent, I had had at least ten different roommates and knew how to do all the domestic jobs. In 1967, working wives were still expected to do housework, and I didn't object until after women's liberation. Years later, while I worked on my PhD, David did most of the housework, certainly his fair share.

Within a short time, he informed me that he did not believe in compromise or accommodation because, he said, "no one got what they wanted." David told me he didn't like peanuts. I like peanuts, so I bought them anyway. About two months after our marriage, my maid of honor visited us for the weekend. David insisted that he wanted my peanuts. I refused to tell him where they were; he started screaming at me, "I want those peanuts." So, I gave him the jar of peanuts, totally humiliated. David also told me that he had no peers. Talk about a challenging relationship. A lot of adjustments, for both of us. Like many couples at that time, we were both working, making the same amount of money, $7,000. We lived on David's salary and saved mine to buy a house.

The arguments in those years revolved around intimacy and social life. Every Sunday, my five siblings, eleven aunts and uncles, plus in-laws and cousins, went to my grandmother's farm for a potluck dinner. David had no grandmother, no Sunday dinners. His grandmother had died giving birth to her first child, David's mother Rosemary. David had no cousins his own age, no neighborhood friends, no classmates coming to his apartment, and no girlfriends. To eliminate any chance the students might meet girls, Quigley Preparatory Seminary, his high school, did not have Saturdays off, they had Thursdays off.

I doubt that David ever met any girls in high school. His last home had been his own private cell; he needed space to himself. Not surprisingly, David wanted to stay in the apartment. I don't think he ever went to one of my grandmother's Sunday dinners; my family was too much for him, and Sun Prairie, Wisconsin, was a three-hour drive from Chicago.

More than anything, I wanted intimacy. Being intimate with God hadn't worked for me; I needed a body. I wanted to share my life with David, and I didn't care how. But he did not want to share anything: not bicycling, not going for walks, nor the movies, not his work or my work, not my feelings or his feelings. Hermit monks don't learn how to share. I was glad I'd been single for seven years; I went bicycling by myself. I think it takes a certain kind of woman to marry a monk, especially a hermit monk like David; resilient, resourceful, and insanely loyal.

We went back and forth on the issue of children for another five to ten years. I was ambivalent, frightened of childbirth, and David became more and more adamant about not wanting children. He continued to stand guard over the privacy of our home; he did not like people in our home, still his cell. I taught half-time, took doctoral-level courses, and dragged David to plays. He quite soon learned to like them—we hardly missed a single theatrical production in Chicago and regularly went to Stratford, Ontario, for the Shakespeare Festival, and the Guthrie Theater in Minneapolis. We saw plays in London frequently. We were both adventuresome and had early decided we wanted to go to Russia before McDonald's got there. We made it; we were always trying to stay ahead of McDonald's.

In spite of all this activity, I found it difficult to maintain a sense of identity being married to an ex-monk, someone who could never make up his mind whether he wanted to be a monk or be married to me. What was our relationship? Not father, not brother, not boyfriend, not quite husband. And, who am I in this relationship? A monk mate? Not exactly a wife, a girlfriend?

Certainly not a mother. What does married mean? Before marrying my ex-monk, I had a stable sense of identity: spinster, professional, member of a multigenerational family, and Catholic. After marrying my ex-monk, I frantically looked around for a social identity suited to my ex-monk husband. I flipped around for five or six years. Then finally, I gave up getting the approval of my ex-monk husband and decided to build my own separate identity.

Then, women's liberation happened, and I was absolutely ready for it. Ms. magazine started in 1971, and by 1973, I stood by our mailbox waiting for the next copy. I went on the birth-control pill with David's disapproval. We had been using the Catholic method of birth control, called rhythm, which meant that we never could have sex at a time when I could get pregnant. This birth-control required me to take my temperature regularly. Even though, I was never sexually satisfied, I took pleasure in his satisfaction. My new sexual aggressiveness, I think, frightened him, and his testosterone level was low. He stopped engaging sexually at this time, continuing to follow the Catholic Church's teaching. This choice created the biggest obstacle in our relationship.

I sublimated, and by 1975, I started deadly serious work on a PhD and dropped the issue of children. In 1981, I won a fellowship to the Folger Shakespeare Library in Washington, DC. I took it and stayed there. At this time, we both were totally focused on work. David still lived in Chicago, continuing to work at Continental Bank, and I lived in Washington.

Although we both complained about needing a wife, this was a very good marriage for both of us. As long as we were not together, I could tolerate the lack of physicality. We did extremely well living in different cities, even different states, and traveling in different countries. We talked on the phone every day and got together every three weeks or so. We had our work lives. I built a good professional network, and David went up the bureaucratic ladder, quickly becoming senior vice president of human resources. When Continental Bank had a major crises, it became the first bank too big to fail; the Feds took it over in 1984, putting in their own management. Perks disappeared as did employees. Reporting to the chairman of the board, David stayed with the bank until he had relocated his direct reports and terminated five thousand other employees without a single lawsuit. He resigned in 1987 to start his own executive consulting business in Washington, DC.

Finally, we were again living together at 415 Independence Avenue SE, just a few blocks from the Folger Shakespeare Library. Difficult adjustment. Since David did not want to go to parties nor did he like my friends stopping by at the end of the Folger workday, my social life was disrupted. Because he was so charming, my friends did not understand why I wasn't accepting invitations to parties. At other times, he was so rude to my friends that they did not want to come to the house. More disruptions. A city water main flooded our basement shortly before our first DC Christmas. I was so depressed that David asked what he could do. I said, "I want a Christmas sing-along." That was the first of our twenty-five Christmas sing-alongs; we were both at our best during sing-alongs. We were good hosts. David always said, "Let's get plenty of food for all the guests." David loved to sing and had a great voice—I just loved to sing, usually off pitch. A friend wrote to me when David was dying, "The most important part of the sing-alongs was the Maguires. . . . Your happy, intense, and joyful presence—both of you (how amazing and wonderful to be able to have THAT all the time) just spread out to each and every one of us."

In spite of our splendid and gracious sing-alongs, monkhood threaded through our life, woven into the fabric, sometimes dominating, sometimes barely visible. Frequently during the decades I lived with David, this thread dominated, sometimes for a week, a month, even years. Easter, David's favorite feast, frequently prompted the emergence of my husband the monk. On one Easter, probably seven or eight years after we were married, Helen, a roommate from graduate school, was visiting us, and she and I were making plans for the day. Sitting in a chair reading a monkish book, David refused to join us and loudly announced that nothing is worth doing, everything is straw. He may have been reading Thomas Aquinas's 1272 famous comment about his *Summa Theologia* being straw. Helen suggested that I not let him talk like that anymore. I followed that advice, probably unwisely.

When his mother died after six months of being in hospice care, David again retired, stopped being a CEO, and again considered going back to the monastery. When he sold his business, he was locked into a non-compete clause; he sat in his favorite green chair in our back parlor reading a lot of monastic-type books. He was not willing to socialize at all. Nor to have a conversation with me. Sex was not even discussed by this time. All of this was very difficult—I did not know if he would go back to the monastery or not. Imagine being a married woman whose husband has intermittent affairs. That is somewhat like being married to an ex-Carthusian. You never know when he will run off and decide to go back to the Charterhouse. I kept telling him to just go so I would have time to start a new life.

In the meantime, I completely focused on work, total sublimation. This went on for about two years. During this time, I began intensive psychotherapy, three times a week, to eradicate the convent nightmares and to learn how to navigate this difficult relationship. I was finally able to actually remember what had happened in the convent and gradually freed myself from convent nightmares. I also learned how to negotiate and accommodate. I told David, "I will never leave you, but I will keep trying to make you more human." Finally, I told David to give it up; no monastery would take him: "You are overweight and out of shape." His ambivalence was never resolved, but, eventually, he found a way to be a monk while being married to me. I felt safer in the marriage and continued to reach out for other resources. We continued to travel a lot: David for business and I for research. We even traveled together sometimes. We began to function as a couple, continuing adventuresome travel: China, Hong Kong several times, Japan, Indonesia, and even Vietnam.

By 1996 David could work remotely as a life coach. I had tired of being an academic scholar; I read Donald Hall's *Life Work* and decided I wanted a writerly life like that, sunup, sundown. We both were ready for a quiet, contemplative life. David found a home for us in the Allegheny Mountains. Our new house was in the middle of eighty acres, mostly forest, mostly black walnut trees. I needed the trees, which have always been my friends. I am a proud Ent, one of Tolkien's tree protectors. David had his monastery, and I had a perfect place to write. Amazing as it seems, we lived there for years without arguing at all, except for bickering about David's addiction to every single sport on TV.

In this tranquil time, I decided to write *An Infinity of Little Hours,* a book about David's life as a Carthusian monk. I had mentioned his monk life at an academic conference, and, to my amazement, I had the floor for two hours. Clearly, a hot topic. David was absolutely essential to my writing the chapter "Monks Off Pitch." A Carthusian novice had emailed me all the liturgical complications of Christmas Night Office; I knew all the steps of this ceremony, but, I needed the music and enlisted David. Remembering choir practice forty years earlier, he was frustrated all over again. He still kept trying to find the right song, the right Christmas carol, to illustrate the Carthusian intervals. As I remember, we kept working on this chapter for weeks with David trying to get perfect examples of the intervals. I kept singing Christmas carols, off pitch, and writing all this down.

David was a huge help to all my writing—his contemplative experience tuned into the rhythms of writing: he became my best critic, my best fan, and my best coach. More generally, David knew how to prepare me for speeches, to stop me from over preparing, letting me know when I was ready to give the speech. He had as good a sense of the rhythms of writing as he had of the contemplative life. I used the top floor of the house, and David had an office on the first floor; he spent his time meditating, reading monastic books, making business phone calls, doing crossword puzzles, playing golf, generally being very content and happy.

As was I. Not only did I have a perfect writing space, but David bought me a Steinway B concert grand. I could play my piano, hike in the mountains, surf the internet, and interview people for my current book about monks. We made several trips to Europe to interview monks and ex-monks. I had plenty of land for gardens and tried to start a vegetable garden, hoping to live off the land. Defeated by mice, chipmunks, deer, and finally bear, I gave up on the garden and started working on the house, supervising construction projects; David patiently tolerated all the mess. We were both happily living together, very content with our life.

What was good about our relationship was so good that our friends envied us. We would each go off in our own direction, gain more skills, learn more, but then we always came back to the center—us. Change kept us together. Six months before he died, David wrote to me, "I look at our forty-seven years together not as a marriage, a quasi-legal act, but as a relation that constantly stretches, strains, and grows. In that regard, I firmly believe our best days are now."

We had very different strengths and interests, and when we worked together, we were invincible. At least, we thought we were, confident that if we worked together we could tackle and solve any problem. We invented new ways of being together.

We kept re-creating our relationship: we lived apart before it was fashionable, and we had separate lives. It worked very well for forty-six years. But, all the energy, strength, and skills of both of us could not beat cholangiocarcinoma, bile duct cancer.

I learned that his death was also the death of "us," our team. The team was not David, not Nancy: the team was a relationship of shared history: a private language, private jokes, common crises, piles of scrapbooks meaningless to anyone else. We were never afraid of a new idea, whether a theological or philosophical challenge. We could count on each other's strengths—even when we were in different states or different countries. We were each other's backboards, companions, and entertainment: two finely honed, but different minds crashing against each other. We played off each other, lived off our exchange, whether practicing our shtick or facing the unbearable together. No matter what each of us did or where we went, we always came back to center, to this relationship.

What held us together? If we were two juxtaposed circles, a Venn diagram, there would be very little intersected space: travel, real estate, and books, but different books. We both had a relentless commitment, high intelligence, high standards, social skills, and shared values. We were usually on the same page, singing the same tune, but often in different keys, sometimes half a note off. We were both thinkers and analyzers, but I was also a feeler.

I'm struggling to find what held us together, to find what we had in common. I find it hard to find words for the extraordinarily deep bond that held us together, no matter what. The relationship was so layered, and we were so grown together, that it is difficult to separate the strands, to parse the relationship. David died seven years ago, making the task both more difficult and easier. He would add a lot to the discussion, but at least he can't spar with me about what I say. The survivor gets to tell the story. Yet, sometimes I know exactly what he would add. When we got the death sentence, Dom Leo, one of the five young men in *An Infinity of Little Hours,* wrote to me, "You will always be where David is. Time and space are the least important aspects of a relationship ." I firmly believe he exists, that we exist. And maybe he cannot forget me.

2

CROSSING TO DEATH

David had wanted to be old from the moment I met him; he hugely admired the old monks who glowed from the inside. He also really wanted to live in a retirement home. Perhaps he was thinking of his parents, perhaps he was thinking of my multiple illnesses. Retirement homes seemed to me like a convent. He dragged me to several, three or four, and each time, I hated them. The interview person would say, "She's not ready for it." David was. Eventually, even I realized we needed a bolt hole, a place to go when one of us got really sick. By 2010, we had decided to sell our home in DC and live in our mountain home full-time, but, there was absolutely no home healthcare in the area. I negotiated. If the retirement home were on the ocean, I would consider it. He didn't have any luck finding one, but he eventually found a brand-new retirement home being built on Lake Michigan. If you can't see across the lake, it is an ocean. I agreed to take a look at it.

We bought into this almost-on-an-ocean place, near my Wisconsin family. David referred to this retirement home as a Sheridan Hilton with a nursing home at the other end. Perhaps best, we were lucky enough to get the penthouse apartment and could design it somewhat as we wished. From my point of view, most importantly, there was a swimming pool with a posh locker room and a gym; from David's point of view, there was underground parking. We expected to live there perhaps four months a year, during the worst of the mountain winter when snow and ice blocked our driveway.

We arrived in Milwaukee on August 26, 2011, exactly five weeks after I had breast cancer surgery at Johns Hopkins, six months after a diagnosis of systemic rheumatoid arthritis. David pushed me into the retirement home in my transfer chair. For the next four years, I kept being pushed around for one reason or another. We had planned to return to our mountain home in two months. I returned five years later.

We had moved eight times in our marriage, but this one was a challenge. We had always had separate office space, usually on separate floors. Suddenly both of us were working in back-to-back offices. I needed quiet, and David did his business calls as if he were talking to a five-hundred-person audience. We stumbled around, trying to find our own space, both in the apartment and the new environment. The penthouse apartment had a 280° view of Lake Michigan, a concierge, and even a chapel. A medical center with an assisted living floor were at the other end of the Hilton.

The new apartment was slow in shaping itself. It did not

help that our furniture was late coming from Washington, DC; when it finally came, forty-seven pieces were either totally smashed or needing repair. Our heavy walnut dining room table was missing a leg, but we found it in the drawer of our dresser, which lacked a foot. A spiral leg of a decorative chair went missing and had to be re-carved. I love telling stories and this was yet one more.

David worked at the difficult job of getting insurance payments from the movers, and I looked for craftsmen who could repair our antique furniture. I found them, finally, but we didn't get the repaired furniture back until nine months later. In the meantime, stacks of books propped up tables and chairs. We always traveled with lots of books. Our most prized possession came through without a scratch: a very heavy and decorated sea chest, which my great-grandparents had used to move from Bohemia to Wisconsin.

Most people in the retirement home were born and bred in Milwaukee and knew the city and its population. Luckily, Eva and Fred, another couple from DC, were moving in at the same time. After living in Washington, D.C., for thirty years, we also felt a bit like immigrants. My great-grandmother probably kept thinking, "We've got to make it to Wisconsin." After my unplanned breast cancer surgery in July, I kept thinking, "We've got to make it to Milwaukee." David claimed he "slung me over his shoulder and made it to the goal line." He was trying to find a place for me to be more fully myself, even though physically handicapped. He felt he had found a safe place for me, one where I could have a social life without him. David hated social life, but he always took extremely good care of me, in fact, he liked taking care of me.

To our vast delight, a peregrine falcon lived on our roof. He sat on the iron railing of our glass balcony, grabbing the railing with his sharp orange talons. Although the fastest animal on earth, he stayed steady and stared straight at me as I took pictures of him. I shared the pictures and the story with the other residents who were quite jealous. David loved the way Milwaukee was laid out, so logically, and we found the people extraordinarily friendly. Our Milwaukee apartment was a great distraction but did not make me forget about my breast cancer. Within a week of our arrival, I checked into the local research hospital for radiation treatment. After checking with my Hopkins radiologist, I found that while I was on methotrexate, an RA drug, radiation could burn my lungs out. I cancelled. Instead of radiation, we chose to use a medical oncologist, a doctor who treats cancer through therapies. We found one recommended by Hopkins in Madison. He prescribed aromatase inhibitors. That option appeared to be simple, if not totally safe.

Wisconsin seemed to be Maguire-friendly, a return to our Midwest roots. To my delight, we had lots of Wisconsin company. Helen, my roommate from graduate school, came to see us very quickly and often, helping to wheel me around. Beatrice, my best friend from grade school, and Janie a roommate from college, lived in Milwaukee and welcomed me back. One of my sisters and her significant other came and helped me unwrap our china, weirdly not broken. Janie drove me around the city, made sure we went to the Downing movie theater where we had gone to foreign films, and to the Milwaukee repertory theater, which we had religiously attended when it was the Fred Miller Theater. Now, Janie and I assiduously watched Rogers and Hammerstein movies in our apartment. David kept going to Glorioso's, the local Italian deli, bringing home gyros and lots of gelato, which our guests ate on the balcony overlooking the Milwaukee Harbor. It was a good time.

My brother Peter set up my great-grandfather's clock in our new apartment; the clock was so old that no one but Peter could figure out how to make it work. It kept ticking. The steadiness of the ticking comforted me while it drove David somewhat crazy. It reminded him of how quickly time was passing; it reminded me of my family history. In September, my entire family had a welcome home dinner for me in our Sun Prairie, Wisconsin, hometown. It was the first one in years. In spite of Thomas Wolfe's *You Can't Go Home Again*, I thought I might have come home. David, never strong on family celebrations, was glad to return to the retirement home in Milwaukee.

We joined the University Club which we could see from our dining room window. It became a very good place for business and for meeting the Marquette people. David loved having breakfast there. We became good friends with the breakfast waiter who always brought David two eggs sunny side up, lots of toast, and hash browns—very heavy on calories. I had hand-squeezed grapefruit juice, a muffin, and fresh fruit while I looked critically at his hash browns. I loved the view from the dining room: the Milwaukee Art Museum with Calatrava's stunning wings, moving out when the museum opened and back in when it closed.

After my decision not to do radiation, I thought my health issues were resolved, but my brushes with death were just starting, and we had no medical network in Milwaukee. In late October, I became so tired I could barely walk. David battled my new internist ferociously, practically coming to blows. David insisted I needed to see an endocrinologist. He was right: I had adrenaline insufficiency, caused by overdosing on prednisone for undiagnosed RA. I was wiped out for a very long time, delaying our return to the mountains.

Meantime, in spite of the medical distractions, we remained upbeat and cheerful. Our friend Eva wanted to start a business creating portraits. I volunteered David as the first subject. He was not happy about it, but he posed. He kept up with his clients and recruited new ones, using the University Club for meetings. When not working, he stood by the elevator and made a point of meeting everyone, knowing their names, and what interested them. He told everyone he was running for mayor. He and two other men bought a Ping-Pong table, and David quickly became the Ping-Pong champion of the retirement home.

When healthy enough, I went to the professional musical events in the retirement home. The Milwaukee Symphony is close to the retirement home, and residents sponsored many solo performances. I particularly appreciated the ancient choral music from a group called Early Music Now. And I loved meeting all the new people. When I returned to the events after a bout of illness, everyone beamed when I walked into the event.

By December, our 280-degree view of Lake Michigan with its wraparound glass balcony, became a challenge. The wind off the lake whipped around our apartment, tossing our lawn furniture around on the balcony, making the apartment very cold. I'm always cold, but this apartment was cold even for David. He still got up very early, by my standards, at least, and turned on our gas fireplace. He did his usual Carthusian meditation in front of the fireplace as he had done in front of the stove in his monastic cell. By the time I got up, the apartment was warm, and I could eat breakfast right in front of the fireplace. Although frightened by my continuous health issues, I thought we were settling into Milwaukee. I believed I was safe.

For our first Christmas in Milwaukee, we invited my entire Wisconsin family, including nieces and grandnephews. We bought about eight roasted chickens from Glorioso's; everyone brought something. I jealously guarded all the chicken bones to make broth, a family tradition. I had great fun showing the grandnephews around the place, and, of course, we had a sing-along, our twenty-fourth. As usual, I sang loudly and enthusiastically, always slightly off pitch, in David's words "in the cracks." Everyone else sang really well. My great-grandmother had included some songbooks in her sea chest, and music seemed to be bred in our bones. There were three professional musicians at our family sing-along, four including David. Things were looking good for returning to Wisconsin. I felt I was finally returning home after being away since I was sixteen.

We had not yet had any serious arguments. Now, once again, inevitably, we sparred over turf. Again, over *An Infinity of Little Hours: Five Young Men and Their Trial of Faith in the Western World's Most Austere Monastic Order*, published in 2006. David was one of the five young men. He kept telling me, people want to talk to the astronaut, not the person who wrote the book. He belittled writing the book, while claiming the credit for being a monk.

For over thirty years, I had strenuously rejected David's monastic life, thinking it a sign of poor mental health. By the time we were in our sixties, I had changed my mind. I was less afraid of my own convent experience and felt safer in our marriage. I was able to reevaluate that part of his life, which had frightened me, both in terms of his emotional stability and his perseverance in our marriage. To convince him I had finally accepted his monk life, I wrote *Infinity*.

Yet, David had absolutely believed no one could capture the life of a Carthusian monk. He told me over and over again, "It is impossible. You can't do that; you will fail." I suspect he may have wanted me to fail. Actually, everyone thought it was impossible to capture the interior life of monks who never spoke, never communicated. Although Carthusian monks were his turf, he wasn't much help with research. He remembered only two things: he loved being in cell and he hated choir. After I had interviewed thirty-some monks, he hated that I knew more about the Carthusian order than he did. Yet, by June 2014, during a talk he gave his colleagues, he referred to the book as "Nancy's love letter to me." He was right. I wrote *Infinity* for him.

Shortly after our Christmas sing-along, I had another weird illness. My energy was so depleted I could not even talk for twenty minutes without breaking into sweats, but I insisted that I had to have some fun. David found a board game in the building, but even five minutes of a simple Monopoly game wiped me out. This illness was the closest David came to losing it, terrified I was going to die. Every Milwaukee doctor we consulted said it was a virus that would cure itself. This siege continued for three months. I was in sweats all night long, drenched; David would take my sodden nightgowns and put them in the dryer. I would put on a dry one which immediately was drenched with sweat. We both thought I was dying. I was ready to die, so tired of being sick and having no hope I would ever feel well again. As I lay in bed, David shouted at me, "Don't die. Don't die," as he grabbed both my feet. We seemed to be crossing to death rather than safety.

After extensive tests, and pages of results, my Madison medical oncologist, the one doctor in Wisconsin we trusted at this time, gave a clear-cut diagnosis. Not entirely safe. The doctor frankly explained, "The meds I prescribed are making you sick." He took me off all of them, promising to personally check me out every three months to look for cancer growth. He explicitly said, "if there is more sign of cancer, you'll need a mastectomy immediately." Three-month checkups involved a lot of trips to Madison, but I enjoyed staying with a sister in Sun Prairie. It was a very slow recovery. I started walking two minutes a day, increasing by another two minutes every week. When I got to twenty minutes a day, I was ecstatic, but David was anxious, exhausted, not feeling entirely safe. He went to the mountains for a break, disappointed I was not going with him. As usual, he wanted to put me in his pocket. I was happy to continue adding a few minutes to my walk.

While David was gone, I started doing some writing. I didn't have the energy to get back to my work-in-progress about my convent experience, but I researched my great-grandparents' voyage from Bohemia to Wisconsin. I hugely admired my great-grandmother who brought a five-week-old baby with her as they crossed the North Sea in late November. When I needed a break, I walked around the retirement home and checked things out. One day, I went to the assisted living quarters on the third floor, looked into an empty room, and realized I would probably die in one of these rooms. That seemed all right. To die here on the shore of Lake Michigan seemed fine to me. I loved being alone in our apartment, no stress, no anxiety. Quiet. Or, as the monks would say, *"Quies."*

By mid-June, David was back. I insisted we start marriage counseling to which he reluctantly agreed. And, I was well enough to go ahead with planning a party for the Milwaukee version of July 4, which is celebrated on July 3. The fireworks were set off in the harbor in front of our apartment. We were ready for the fireworks on our wraparound balcony, the best viewing place in the entire city. Eva and Fred, the other couple from DC, and myself thought the fireworks magnificent, incredible, better than the ones at the DC Capital. We packed the balcony with people from the retirement home. In a picture I took of this group, people I thought would be dead in a year are still alive, and the healthiest, including David, are dead. Magnificent fireworks are very frequent and very loud in Milwaukee. I loved the constant sense of celebration and wished I could join the crowds, but David hated the noise. After a while, we both preferred quiet to fun.

During this party, I had trouble breathing; I blamed it on my usual allergies, but in 2012, the air pollution in Milwaukee was the worst in the United States. I had to go to the ER for oxygen. David used all his persuasive powers to find a pulmonologist. Unfortunately, the new pulmonologist, also new to this hospital, put me on medication that made my voice box swell. I lost my voice for months. By threatening to leave the hospital system for a private pulmonologist, David forced the pulmonology department to eventually give me a pulmonologist specializing in asthma. Our first appointment lasted five hours. David stayed with me for these long appointments and eventually the diagnosis was clear. I had asthma. My asthma doctor quickly became my most trusted doctor in Milwaukee.

In David's words, our team had diminished to one and one half. One train went out, another came in. David pointed out that we did not have one solid week without a medical emergency. Neither of us felt we had passed to safety. David started as a LPN, a licensed nurse practitioner, taking care of my getting in and out of bed, my food, my mobility, carting me to doctor appointments and forcing doctors to see me when they didn't have time. He did an exceptional job managing the plethora of specialists, usually five or six. He struggled to find the best doctors for me and would not accept their claim that they had no time, and by sheer will power, and skill, coerced them into seeing me. I promoted him to the chief medical officer, a CMO. He appreciated the promotion.

As long as David had my back, I was never frightened. I would push my transfer chair around the lobby so I could sit down when I got tired. When I met someone, I would say, "Let's talk quickly before something else happens. I will probably have skin cancer tomorrow." Within a few days, I was diagnosed with basal skin cancer. When not doing his CMO work, David kept playing Ping-Pong, continuing his consulting business, looking for new clients, usually pro bono. He enjoyed working with young entrepreneurs. The other residents admired our humor and good spirits in tackling all these problems.

Although I could not talk, I could certainly eat. We celebrated our forty-fifth wedding anniversary at the best restaurant in Milwaukee, Sanford's. We had never been there, but everyone talked about it. We found it located in a corner house, a few blocks away. A valet immediately rushed out to park our car. We got there early and had the place to ourselves with lots of attention from the staff. They created a special dessert for us with the year forty-five written on it. David was enjoying every minute; he had put on a suit, and even allowed the staff to take a picture of us. I glowed. I wore my most flamboyant red dress; it looked as if it came from China with lots of intricate patterns and colors. I justified the purchase by telling David that I was buying it for my funeral. I saved it, and I might just wear it for my funeral. We enjoyed ourselves as much as we had anywhere.

We congratulated ourselves for coping well with the move and all my illnesses. We were back to our real selves, we were again Nancy and David. I could live without a voice, and we saw no problems in our near future. How could there be such a restaurant in Milwaukee, as good as anything in New York? And what fun to live in a small city. We were jubilant. We had such a glorious time we decided we would celebrate something every month. That was our last trip to Sanford's.

Days later, I had a fever of 102 degrees, which lasted for twelve days. My CMO kept taking me to different doctors, but they all claimed it was a virus, and nothing could be done medically. David insisted that I be referred to an ENT; a CT scan clearly showed my maxillary sinus totally blocked with a fungal infection. That diagnosis put all of the neighbors who were physicians into play. An infectious disease doctor and his wife were a major support. In January 2013, I had sinus surgery, which eventually led to the end of high fevers—and the end of my life-threatening medical problems.

We had out-Jobed Job. David saved my life at least three times during this medical marathon. We coped as we had for forty-six years. I had a sense of dark humor. David, in charge of God, had an unconscionable faith; he was so thick with God that I counted on his influence in another place. When David was on the job, I always felt safe and fearless. He loved taking care of me and was very good at it. He had plenty of opportunity. And he didn't have time to do much else besides caring for me. When I was ill, I was happy to have him in charge. No arguments. He was in total charge of everything, even me. As fragile as I was, and exhausted, I felt very emotionally stable.

We were ninety-nine percent certain I would die first. I never feared death because I knew David would be with me. I had the "get out of jail free" card. Both of us felt the survivor had the truly difficult job. I would have been happy to die before David, or with him. David varied on his plans if I died first. First, he said it would not make any difference to him at all if I died. Later, he said he planned to stay in our apartment for a year or two thinking of our life together and what we had accomplished.

Our plan was absolutely solid. David was resilient and healthy, and I was a contender for the most chronic diseases in the Golden Olympics. David planned to take care of me until I died. Never, never, did we think that David would die first. I could not even imagine taking care of a dying David. Impossible.

3

ON MY OWN

ONE DAY, David had a pain in his side, possibly due to kidney stones or to Ping-Pong, which I always thought he played excessively. His internist ordered a CT scan which revealed not muscle strain or kidney stones but lesions in his liver.

Our first liver meeting was on with Douglas Evans, MD, the head of the cancer center, and a highly credentialed and respected physician. He compared the images taken a year earlier when David had benign lesions with the current images and told us "the lesions are growing." He explained that the cancer was multifocal. The term went right over our heads, we did not have a clue what he meant. He recommended a surgeon, a relatively young man eager to make his mark, a bit of a cowboy. Craig immediately took charge of David's case, ordering a vast variety of tests: an eight-hour biopsy, MRIs, PET scans, and every other kind of scan—nine doctor appointments during Holy Week. For the first time in decades, even I was very aware of Good Friday. The day after my surgery for skin cancer on my lower eyelid, on March 28, 2013, David was diagnosed with liver cancer. My eye doctor had said that I could not get any moisture on the incision, but I couldn't stop crying. David called the doctor and said, "she must cry." The doctor agreed the tears would not hurt my incision.

The tests did not determine the source of the liver cancer, and the biopsy sample was not large enough to be predictive. We thought and analyzed, as always, and decided, at the very least, that surgery would provide a larger sample of the cancer. Craig had told us the odds of survival from the surgery were ninety-nine percent.

We were low on emotional resources—my own medical events had exhausted us—but we had no choice but to go forward, immediately. David's surgery was set for April 12. We were not in a major panic. This was David's third cancer, the first two being prostate cancer, and we had caught the liver cancer very early. David was totally nonchalant about the surgery. He was good at denial and was convinced that all he would feel would be the intravenous needle. His main concern was with me. After the fungal infection surgery in January, I was still running a recurring fever, peaking at 102 degrees.

On the day of the surgery, via cell phone, Craig reported that during a six-hour J-cut surgery, he had removed two lesions, portions of the bile ducts, and all of the gallbladder. A smaller lesion was burned off. While he was talking to me, his residents were sewing up David. Reassuring me, Craig promised that in an emergency, he would be there. Unfortunately, and naively, I failed to ask him for his cell phone number. Glad it was over, I was guardedly optimistic—it might be all right.

Concerned about my sinus infections, David had preregistered me with the retirement home's medical center. During his surgery, I could, if needed, automatically check into the center. David also reserved a guest apartment for a member of my family and her partner, asking them to be available during his surgery, especially at 9 p.m., when I took a precisely timed medication.

The day after the surgery, I felt feverish and tired and went to bed at 4 p.m. When I woke about 9 p.m., my entire body was shaking, after a while, when I realized my relative was not coming, I called a new friend, Mary Beth, who found my temperature 102°. Mary Beth called the medical center who contacted my relative who arrived, saying, somewhat angrily, "you can't blame this on us." My mind doesn't work very well at 102°, but I clearly remember saying, "David said you should be here until 9 p.m." I don't remember saying anything else.

The incident, whatever it was, ended my relationship with this woman. The arrangement had not worked, perhaps a misunderstanding, a failure of empathy, maybe both. Our family was not tightly bound; family riffs have lasted over a decade. This one was surprising. She and I had been close during her divorce and subsequent relationship, and was the first person I called to report David's cancer. Mary Beth left, and I was alone in my bedroom, somewhat frightened. I was beginning to be aware of what my life would be without David.

The next morning, my fever remained, and I checked into the medical center. David would be discharged from the hospital directly to the medical center, and I would be there to take care of him. Even though the medical center required I have some tests, I felt as if I were on vacation. I had some necessary quiet time, with three meals a day, and visits from Helen and concerned neighbors.

David's main danger was infection, and my fever kept me from visiting him. Mary Beth, a nurse at the hospital, regularly checked on him and reported her observations. He was too weak to speak on the phone, and incoherent when he tried. Eight days after the surgery, Mary Beth told me they were thinking of discharging him. When I called the hospital, his on-duty nurse told me that his white count was off; she also did not think he was ready to be discharged. I objected to the discharge, but he arrived later that day. Only later did I find out that I could have stopped the discharge.

David came home extremely weak, incoherent, and in a lot of pain; the bumpy ride from the hospital had not helped. I managed to get him into a wheelchair and took him to his room in the skilled care section of the medical center. For over an hour, he sat in his wheelchair, not speaking, just holding my hand. He finally said in a very low and weak voice, "I'm still here." I heard, "I have not left you." Much later when we talked about it, he said, "That is what I meant." Then he said slowly, with deep relief, "It is so good to be with humans."

When the nurse finally came, he was too weak to respond. For the first time in our marriage, I answered questions directed to David. Eating dinner with him, I encouraged him to "just shove it in." He tried, I tried, but his throat was very sore, and the food was very awful. He seemed to brighten up when the physical therapist came and started doing exercises with him.

I continued to stay in the room across the hall from David. I checked on him before I went to bed, and the nurse stopped later to tell me he had asked to walk in the hallway, a good sign. Thinking he was okay, I went to sleep. Because I was not in his room, I didn't know he had called for help during the night, writhing, confused, and unable to get out of bed. The LPN told him he would have to wait until breakfast to get help, not calling the RN on the second floor. By breakfast time, he was weak, incoherent, his pulse oximeter reading low, his blood pressure alarming. By 9:00 a.m. on Sunday, nineteen hours after he had arrived, the charge nurse, a pool nurse, came to me and said, "we don't know what is wrong. Your husband needs to go back to the hospital. Get a car." A neighbor and his wife came immediately.

In a very low and feeble voice, David kept telling me how sorry he was. I said with anguish, "You have nothing to be sorry about." He apologetically and miserably said, "You take such good care of me." Before we left for the hospital, an aide checked David's vitals. I asked her to check his pulse oximeter reading. She said she thought he had enough oxygen to get to the hospital. I yelled, "You think he has enough." The charge nurse was chatting with someone, and after what seemed a long wait, we left with an oxygen tank in the car. David struggled to keep up a conversation, until I begged him to save his energy. Then, he sat silently, uncomfortably, hating to go back to the hospital.

The charge nurse had preregistered him on a hospital floor instead of the ER. After I signed the paperwork at 9:30 a.m., the neighbors left to return the oxygen tank, and David and I were left on our own. I had never been in this hospital; it seemed much larger than the familiar Johns Hopkins Hospital. So many people were walking around. Instead of being in a room, David's bed was shoved in the hallway, on an unfamiliar floor. He needed immediate care. His J-cut incision was still raw, only eight days old. I grabbed a nurse, who found his blood pressure above 200, his temperature 102.4, his breathing very irregular and shallow. The nurse did not say a doctor would come. She disappeared, and nothing seemed to be happening. I did not know what was going to happen next. I repeatedly said, "Call his surgeon; he said he would be here in an emergency." The surgeon, Craig, did not show up until a week later.

Looking around, I saw patients watching TV, reading books, and talking to nurses and doctors while David was in the hall unattended. Flagging every person in a white coat, I tried desperately to get their attention, but no one listened to me or even paid attention to the patient in the hallway. David kept pleading, "Don't leave me," and I was emotionally unable to leave him to get help. David was in trouble, and I was not able to protect him. I failed to get help. In those hours, forty-six years of safety, of trust, disappeared. Agonizingly incompetent and impotent, I was unable to help the person who was my entire world. That sense of impotence became familiar and more intense in the months to follow.

Finally, at nearly 1:00 p.m., a tall, dark-haired man in a white coat appeared. He asked me about our medical directive. I told him our directive was in the hospital's medical record; he then asked me about heroic measures. I hesitated. How serious was David's condition? He then went to ask David, who turned to me and said, "That is what you want, isn't it?" With tears streaming down my face, I nodded, agreeing to do anything to keep David alive. I wanted them to take all measures. As they wheeled David away to the SICU, the surgical intensive care unit, the most intense form of care in the hospital, he turned to me and said, "See you soon."

Forty-five minutes later, I was allowed into his SICU cubicle, David was already unconscious. An IV was pumping the standard antibiotic, meropenem, into him. I had no reason to believe this was a deadly illness. I was confused. I did not know what was wrong with him, but, he was getting antibiotics. At 5:30 p.m., the ER doctor told me to go home because they would want me back at 7:30 a.m. I begged with my voice breaking, "Please don't let him die. Call me if something goes wrong."

Very worried, I returned to my room in the medical center.

After dinner, using every imaging technique I had, I fell asleep. About 1:00 a.m., the LPN woke me to ask, "Do you blame me for what happened to your husband?" I had no idea what she was talking about. I tried to go back to sleep. At 1:30 a.m., my cell phone rang. It was the SICU doctor. She said, "Your husband is bottoming out. Come at once." The LPN had locked up my meds and didn't know how to open the cabinet, so I left without them. The neighbors who had driven the day before came immediately; the streets were empty, there was no traffic, and we arrived very quickly. I realized he could be dead, but I wasn't crying, not feeling any emotion at all. The hospital was in lockdown, but, fortunately, one of my drivers was a lawyer who spoke like God. He said, "This woman's husband is in extremis." The door swiftly opened.

I went straight to David's SICU cubicle. He was still unconscious, breathing irregularly, and much more shallowly, than the night before. He looked indeed as if he were "bottoming out." I don't remember feeling anything, just watched his breathing. My neighbors left about 4:00 a.m. Alone, I kept signing releases, only refusing to sign the ventilator release. Two months earlier, I had used a ventilator during the fungal infection surgery, but under general anesthesia. I insisted David be sedated. He had a low pain threshold, and I was afraid of causing him pain. The nurse said he was too weak to be sedated. I had David's medical power of attorney, and they could do nothing without my written authorization. At 9:00 a.m., the tall man in the white coat who had been waiting to put in a ventilator, came into David's cubicle and desperately shouted at me, "If we don't put in a ventilator, he will stop breathing." I did not understand. I was confused and terrified. Was I signing his death warrant? I did not know what to do. Then . . . I signed.

As I left the SICU, I called my sister who had been a hospice nurse. When she asked how David was, I stammered, "He is unconscious." Shaking with angst and terror, I was crying so hard I could barely talk. She said, "Oh my God, he has septicemia." That was the first time I heard the word. I did not know what it meant.

Another neighbor came to pick me up. After finding me with difficulty, he wheelchaired me to his car and drove me back to our apartment. During the drive, as I sobbed hysterically, relentlessly, the neighbor stared straight ahead, clenching the steering wheel with white knuckles. I went straight to our apartment, determined to never go back to the medical center. My medicine was there, as well as my clothes. But, I didn't want to see the LPN again, I did not trust the staff. I was terrified at the thought of going back. I had not been discharged, yet I could not go back. I would not go back.

David and I were never able to figure out what I did that afternoon. I remember nothing of the afternoon or evening. I didn't leave the apartment. I don't remember what I did, if anything. I was probably in shock. Perhaps I looked out the window at what I called my ocean. I couldn't have listened to my great-grandfather's clock because I had not wound it while I was in the medical center. I really can't remember anything except Mary Beth's telephone calls. I was still crying uncontrollably. She arranged my release from skilled care; Holger, her husband, brought my things from the medical center and tried to persuade me to eat. I did not try to go back to the hospital that day—later, both David and I thought that impossible and odd.

I was too terrified to sleep. I kept my cell phone next to me on the bed. The next morning, Tuesday, when I returned to the SICU, machines filled David's cubicle—so many I could barely find space for myself. I saw a dead David. What looked like white felt, rolls of surgical gauze, covered and kept in place the tubes and needles which were attached to the machines in his room. The only skin visible was his forehead, and it was charcoal gray. His eyes were closed and sunken.

Machines had taken over his body. The only sign of life was a quarter inch of dark brown urine, an image burned into my brain. I maneuvered around the machines so I could hold his hand.

From being David, he had turned into something not quite David, then not even human, and now into a monster. I did not know if he was dying or already dead. Either way, I had to stay with him, hold his hand. I felt as if I knew how the Blessed Virgin felt as she stood at the foot of the cross. I did not know what was wrong with David. I just knew some powerfully evil force had taken over, destroying David, and I could not save him, could do nothing. Worst of all, I had no human contact, no doctors, nurses, or any other source of information. On a terror scale of 1 to 10, I hit far beyond 10. My interior life seemed be subsumed, becoming sheer horror.

That morning, I saw/felt an image of our planet Earth. Everything I valued, and which made sense of human life, was gone. Our planet had turned to ashes; history, literature, theology, philosophy, all the humanities, were being pushed into an endlessly deep crevasse. I was standing alone on this ashen planet, responsible for re-creating it, and I didn't have a stick or twig to rebuild. For forty-six years, David had been with me in crisis, the two of us resolving whatever problem, dreadful times, hard decisions. Now I was facing this terrifying crisis alone. In the worst of times, this image still occurs, and then I know I have reached my psychological limit.

David was too fragile to be moved for a scan. I still knew only that he was dangerously ill. Not until later, on Tuesday night, did the doctors decide it was less risky to move him than to leave him without a diagnosis. The scan showed a liver abscess. Bacteria had entered David's bloodstream during surgery, growing rapidly. Since no doctor or nurse visited either David or me, I had no source of information. The SICU nurse did her best, but protocol did not allow her to talk about

David's diagnosis or prognosis. In this particular hospital, taking care of the family of patients was not a priority.

After a few days of watching David's unconscious body, I angrily and insistently demanded to see a member of David's surgical team. An assistant surgeon and a NP were available for perhaps five minutes. I asked, "Why did you discharge him prematurely?" The surgeon answered, "He wanted to go home." He told me, as if I did not know, that my husband was very sick. I asked for the odds; he said twenty percent that David would die. He had not even been to see David; I don't know if he had a diagnosis then, but statistically he was wrong. When organ failure occurs, the odds are forty to sixty percent, more so in the elderly. David's kidneys had failed, usually one of the first signs of septicemia. David was seventy-five at the time.

My sister had been correct. David had septicemia, an often fatal infection of the blood. Septicemia works very quickly; survival depends on minutes. Several factors contributed to David's near-death: the premature discharge, the LPN not calling a nurse, the perhaps six-hour delay in getting David to the hospital, and the three-and-a-half-hour wait before he was taken to the SICU. The septicemia experience determined our subsequent decisions, our life-and-death decisions. The issue was not about death but about the manner of death. I knew I could not again experience David being put out, being consumed. I feared, knew, I would lose my mind if I saw septicemia shut him down again, turn him into something totally non-David. I would not be able to watch this again. I would absent myself, as I later did.

Twice every day, I continued to go to the hospital, but I was already in PTSD. The seventy days that David was in the hospital/medical center were, and still are, a blur—I updated people on David's condition, signed authorization papers, talked to doctors by phone, and kept visiting David, but everything ran together. After David came safely back, I tried to parse this time: What happened when? What day was it? What day did David turn into a monster, was it my morning visit or afternoon visit?

When I next saw David in the SICU, on Wednesday, he was conscious but still on a respirator. He could not talk, but, with great agitation, he kept trying to engage the nurse. She said, "Can't this wait until tomorrow?" He shook his head. The nurse did not know what he wanted, but he was insisting. And even now, he got what he wanted. She put an immense whiteboard in front of him and gave him a marker. While I was standing next to him, he started writing in huge letters: "When will she come back?" His political instinct was still intact. He knew the nurse was the one in control. I told him I would continue to come twice a day. Morning visit, home for lunch and a short nap, afternoon visit, supper, and to bed for my nightmare movie reel of the monster. This routine did not change for the next month.

On the fifth day, David cheerfully and triumphantly waved at me. His ventilator had been removed, but the drain the surgeon had inserted to collect the fluid coming from the liver abscess was not removed until weeks later. He could talk, was talking, probably about how well he thought he was doing. He didn't understand what had happened to him during the previous week. When the PT people arrived to exercise him, he stopped paying attention to me. I said, "David, would you rather I leave?" He said, "I have work to do." The PT said I could stay, but David observed, "I'll be tired." I asked, "David, do you want me to go?" He said, "Yes." I have never been so happy to be kicked out. He couldn't live without me for four days; now I got kicked out. His nurse and I laughed and danced a jig in the hallway outside the SICU.

On his last morning in the SICU, Friday, David was very upset, hopeless. His SICU nurse had told him he was being transferred to a floor. He had been receiving excellent care, and he knew, and I knew, that kind of care would not continue on a floor. He had totally given up getting the care he needed. He was worried for his life. He was also worried about his inability to communicate with the staff. I said, "I will talk to the team." David said in despair, "No one talks to the team." The SICU nurse offered to tell me when he was transferred. She called me late on Friday and gave me the name of his new floor nurse.

Kathy, our lawyer, was with me in our apartment during my speakerphone conversation with his floor nurse, the same nurse who twelve days earlier had thought David should not be discharged. Kathy took notes. The nurse assured me that David would not be left alone. A nurse would always be with him, and she herself would call me when her shift was up. She did, and the next nurse called me regularly throughout the night. The floor nurse had told us that his surgeon would be making rounds at eight o'clock the next morning. Kathy promised, "I'll pick you up at 7:30 a.m."

In spite of the sleepless night, I was ready for the 7:30 a.m. appointment. As I look back at this time, I wonder how I managed to keep moving, to keep hopelessly trying to do what David had always done for me. To make doctors do what I needed them to do, to make them available to me. I did what I could, but, unlike David, I don't do magic.

We got to the hospital at eight and went straight to David's room. Four days earlier, David was putting out ¼ inch of dark brown urine. Now, he was slumped over in a straight chair in the corner of the room, no nurse in sight, trying to eat some concrete-looking food. He said, painfully and with difficulty, "I need a nurse." The nurse had promised someone would always be with him. How could I possibly manage an institution this large? David's care overwhelmed me. This wasn't like managing building contractors or a scholarly seminar group.

I looked up, and saw Kathy talking to a doctor in the hallway; I recognized David's surgeon. I went out and said, "Hello, Craig, meet Kathy, my friend and lawyer." Then I said, "If you ever discharge him prematurely again, I will go straight to Douglas Evans, the head of the cancer center, then I will go to the newspapers, then to the Supreme Court, if necessary." Craig said, "I really don't think all that is necessary." Then he walked on. During David's time in the hospital, Craig frequently asked David if I really was going to sue him. David did not know.

With the help of Kathy, I hired a specialist to check all of David's records, the standing of the nurses, his current medications, and his charts. Twice a day, I went to his room, highly visible. There were so many specialists in the room, probably six or seven, that there was scarcely space for me. None of them talked to me. Not realizing what had happened to him, David was reacting intuitively, politically. He needed to do well in this strange environment. He did not seem to be aware of my presence, but one day, as I left, he said, *"Courage."* When not in the hospital, I stayed in our apartment, not having the energy to disguise my grief and terror from the other residents. The flashbacks were relentless for weeks, and every morning I woke up exhausted.

The lab work identified David's cancer as cholangiocarcinoma, bile duct cancer. In the Western world, there are one to two cases per 100,000 cancers. Because the cancer has multiple sources, Cholangiocarcinoma is an incurable and rapidly lethal cancer. Nothing will cure it but surgery, but the surgery would have to be almost instantaneous with the beginning of the cancer.

At this time, the diagnosis meant little to me. David's surgeon, Craig, was very excited; this was the first time he had operated on someone with this very rare cancer. Craig was very optimistic about David's prognosis. At this stage I was more concerned about septicemia than cancer. David was not concerned about anything for a very long time.

The monster from *Star Trek*, whom David later called "the metal man," continued to envelop my life and dominate my nights. I slept very little and self-isolated continually. David continued to be David, and nearly dying did not stop him from wanting to be in control of his body, as well as everything else. He kept demanding walks. His cancer doctors were hesitant, but they released him to rehab so he would have more opportunity to take walks. Excited about this, David called to tell me he was going to do SEAL training, in his mind the challenge of Navy seal training. I told David over and over, "Just get a little bit better every day, don't do more than that." But David, being David, thought he was in the Olympics and passed all the SEAL tests in less than a day. He was booted out.

Booted out? When the rehab doctor called to tell me to pick him up. I asked, "What kind of support would I have?" A nurse for fifteen minutes a day? David needed his drain flushed three times a day, meropenem injected intravenously three times a day, for three hours each time. I was supposed to do this? Could I do this? This level of care required a CNA, a certified nursing assistant, at the least. He was not ready to be discharged from the hospital. I refused to accept the discharge. The rehab doctor said to me, "This is the first time I've seen a wife unhappy when her husband gets well." At this point, David spoke up authoritatively and insistently: "I will go to a hotel." Not only am I battling an insane medical system, I'm battling David. With the help of Lisa, the new head of the medical center, I was able to keep him in the hospital through the weekend.

After six days in the SICU and twenty-four in the hospital, David was discharged. The nursing inspector told me David's odds were 50-50 but assured me that he would personally check on his care. Based on this, I had David transferred back to the skilled care center, with the provision that the LPN not get near him. David's case was nearly infamous at the hospital. Before he was discharged, all the specialists met with us. The infectious disease doctor gave me specific instructions on signs of septicemia recurring. She also gave me her cell phone number in case the meropenem had not arrived by 8:00 p.m. When I called the skilled care center to check on the meropenem, they did not have it—they said they had ordered it. I was irate, frantic, asking: "You ordered it? You don't have it?" I was not a casual patient advocate. I was so exhausted I had to ask a neighbor to push me to the medical center, where I inspected the label, checking to be sure they really had meropenem. I had learned not to trust the medical center. Again, I ended the day spent, exhausted.

I was now in the apartment all the time. At first, not going to the hospital twice a day was a relief. I needed the rest. But the flashbacks did not stop, and I was terrified by the uncertainty, the lack of precision, the inability to plan. Would David ever come back? Do I want to stay here alone for the rest of my life? I was terrified of the living room with its wraparound balcony. There was too much space, too much uncertainty and ambiguity. I had no one to call for help. My best friend, David, was still so weak he couldn't talk to me. Suicide was never far from my mind. I needed to get the monster from *Star Trek* out of my mind, forget about the quarter inch of dark brown urine. I seemed to be safer in David's small, enclosed office with no windows. I kept winding my great-grandfather's clock.

David was living in the medical center, safe for the time being. He also was not sleeping well, the staff administered meropenem three times a day, one of the times in the middle of the night. He still hadn't remembered anything of what happened to him. He rarely spoke when I was with him. Much later, he said, "I don't remember seeing you very much in the medical center." Other residents would stop to see him – normally he did not want to see anyone, but he learned to trust one man in particular, Ron. He asked him to go with him to the ER if septicemia returned. David did not understand what had happened to him, nor what was happening now, but he understood I could not watch it again. He slept when they weren't administering meropenem. He had been so weakened by septicemia that there was no possibility of even thinking of another procedure.

During the next weeks, David would ask me, "Are you keeping something from me that's interfering in our relationship?" I would say, "Yes. Do you want me to tell you?" He would turn away from me and then firmly and quietly say, "No." David was not able to process his near-death, his lack of control over his body, and he was extraordinarily weak after weeks of the strongest antibiotic available. He never remembered what happened to him, and I have never forgot.

While attempting to sleep over the next weeks, I relived my experience of David's first death, an endless reel of David turning into a sci-fi monster. I called my local internist for sleeping pills, but his receptionist said he never gave out sleeping pills because they make you groggy during the day. A doctor friend from Washington sent a prescription for 15 mg temazepam, a sleeping pill, with numerous refills. The maximum dose is two. I took as many as three a night. Throughout the following months, I never took a tranquilizer or antidepressant, but lots and lots of temazepam and Imodium.

I had to talk about what I'd seen, how I felt, and David was still too fragile to cope with this harsh reality. The three hundred people in the retirement home were unwilling to listen. Looking back, they were mostly strangers who didn't know me at all. We had been in the city and this retirement home less than two years. Perhaps my despair and terror frightened them. One woman listened, but after I finished my story, she laughed as if I had told a joke. I had adjusted to other institutions but didn't know how to adjust to this one.

I felt totally isolated, in a different world from the residents who were busy going to lunch, dinner, book clubs, to the symphony—unaware or oblivious that my world had changed forever. I sensed I had misjudged the way human beings interact. During my most dangerous years living alone on Capitol Hill, neighbors were looking out for me. Here, I was isolated in my world of grief and terror, afraid of everything, not even trusting my own body.

I called my best friend from graduate school, Helen, who had been with me a week earlier during David's surgery. When she heard my voice, she stopped the conversation and said, "I need to terminate this relationship for the time being. It is too emotional." Helen had terminated our relationship several times before, once with an intermission of several decades. So, that should not have surprised me, but she was the only person who was part of my world, the only one I trusted. All of my assumptions about human relationships seemed to have been wrong.

Finally, Nici, a Jewish neighbor whom I had met only once at a cocktail party, made me promise to call her if I needed help. Hitler had chased her family all around Europe; she was not afraid of terror. So, I called her. With great hesitation, I asked if she would listen to my story. She said "yes" and immediately came to our apartment. She not only tolerated but listened to my anguished, choking voice, and finally I could tell the whole story. She probably saved my life. Our peregrine falcon returned that week.

To protect David if something happened to me, I called David's second power of attorney and asked if I could put his name under mine as the medical power of attorney. With the advice of the infectious disease doctor, I created flyers about the early warning signs of severe septicemia and distributed them to the skilled care staff. I assiduously met with the staff, checked on David, verified the information to be sent with David if he were readmitted to the ER, and continued to write and email updates on David's condition to our family and friends.

But, my stress level was so acute that I called a psychiatrist friend in DC. He unhesitatingly diagnosed PTSD. A good friend of his was slowly dying of severe septicemia, and he understood my anguish very clearly. He made himself available to me 24/7, even when he was hosting a dinner party in his home. The more I was able to talk about what happened, the less terror I experienced, the less weight on my shoulders. Every conversation lifted about fifty pounds.

Yet until I could tell all of this to David himself, the unbearable and terrifying memory kept me secluded in our apartment.

4

REPRIEVE

BY LATE MAY, the radiologist finally said: "It's more dangerous to leave the drain in than to take it out." The drain was removed to David's great delight, but would he survive without it? The radiologist predicted a risk of recurrence from one to four weeks. A week later, the infectious disease doctor decided to stop meropenem, the surefire antidote against septicemia, creating a high risk for a week. I was a wreck, waiting, terrified of septicemia. I circulated a detailed plan of care for David to the medical center staff and neighbors. A group of them stood vigil with me, ready to be with me if David went back to the ER. Everyone understood I would not go back to the ER with David. He was still being monitored but doing all right. His first post-surgical MRI was good. No cancer. No septicemia. Perhaps we were returning to life.

Finally, David could walk back and forth to the apartment from the medical center, the equivalent of about three city blocks in the same building. But after a few hours, he eagerly went back to the familiar security of skilled care. For over two months, he had been living in cell-like hospital rooms and was uneasy about returning to our apartment: too much space with no nurses at hand. He kept visiting, gradually coming earlier, and even staying for lunch. Although he was uneasy about being away from the skilled care nurses, he started to relax. Watching him sleep on the sofa made me think he might still be alive. Quite soon, we were ready to talk about his return. Until he could stay in the apartment for an entire day, I insisted he remain in skilled care. He tried to argue that we could both get well in the apartment, pointing out I had fallen asleep while he was there; apparently, I had felt safe. He was finally able to stay for a day, but later confessed he had thought he had only a fifty percent chance of staying permanently. Extremely good at denial, David, I think, had just blocked out his belief that he couldn't live in the apartment.

David still did not know what happened in the SICU; he did not know he had had severe septicemia. I could not tell him. He had been too weak, had not wanted to know, had resisted the story. Even when we were talking about his hospital stay with his second power of attorney, he quickly broke off from the conversation and watched a TV sports event. He was concerned about our relationship, but until he knew what had happened, he could not possibly understand my uncharacteristic reticent, bottled-up behavior. Until I told David the story, we could not reconnect, could not repair our relationship. Finally, I told him very slowly, and fearfully, in a voice incoherent with terror and anguish. I told him about the emergency trip to the hospital, the long wait in the hospital, his admission to the SICU, his near-death, his weeks of severe septicemia, and my own grief and terror. At first, he was astonished, disbelieving. He was unable to listen to the whole story, too much to understand all at once, so I stopped and finished the following day.

Then, I asked him what he would have done if I were the one in the hall bed. He raged, "I would smash glass, I would break into the ER, I would have left you to get help and save your life." He was extremely angry at me. But I am not David. I do not know how to smash glass. I just persist. He understood. He knew now how close to death he had come, and an enormous burden rolled off my shoulders. After sharing the horror of the experience with David, my world returned. David had been the one I needed to tell. The day after I finished the story, David returned to our apartment.

As soon as he moved his things into the apartment, he got into our shower. I watched in amazement as he showered for fourteen minutes. Enough with sponge baths. A few days later, the air conditioner went off in the apartment. The heat triggered my asthma, and David was still very fragile, still unsure whether he could live in the apartment. I tried to get a guest apartment, but they were already taken. David suggested we try to get a room at the University Club—I pointed out he could not drive and neither could I.

Helpless in the penthouse, we were both too exhausted to even analyze our options, much less walk to the club. We did not feel safe. We were not safe. We had no one looking out for us, and I had nowhere to seek advice. It took a while before either of us felt safe enough to leave the apartment. We were not yet prepared to meet the faces on the elevator. David was no longer confident that he could solve everything or anything, and I was afraid of more rejection, abandonment. We had radically changed, and we had just two old friends in Milwaukee, friends who knew us before this terrifying event. Beatrice was in a nearby suburb with a very ill husband in the hospital. Janie was unwilling or unable to be of help. The people we had entertained in our apartment had disappeared. We were alone.

We were both traumatized and didn't recognize the people we had become. We were so afraid that, to everyone's astonishment, we held hands as we walked around the lobby. We were rarely out together and we had never held hands. Like all PTSD patients, I was afraid of everyone and everything. The worst had happened, and I was braced for whatever else might happen. Four weeks after the drain was removed, we finally had reason to believe septicemia was over, ancient history. David, the optimist, was confident. I was jubilant, but afraid to believe it, just beginning to believe that we might come back to life. A very long and deep massage in the wellness center put me to sleep for what seemed like days. I had one massage after another, until I turned to mush.

David seemed totally ephemeral to me; I thought I could see through him, impossible to believe he was really alive, back in our apartment. To his annoyance, I kept touching him to be sure he really was alive: he had looked so dead in the SICU. He would ask curiously, "Why are you touching me?" When he closed the bathroom door, I feared he would never reappear. I kept looking at him, doubting that he was really there. He would ask with curiosity and perhaps annoyance, "Why are you looking at me?"

But David counted on me being continually on watch, making sure septicemia had not come back. His canary in the coal mine, still on vigil, I needed to stay awake to protect both of us. When awake, I could repress the memory of the ashen earth and the quarter inch of dark brown urine. When I fell asleep, I could not control these images. I failed to sleep.

We began weighing ourselves on the professional scale in the gym. David had lost twenty-two pounds since April 12, and I had lost ten. To my terror/delight/amazement, I was still losing half a pound a week. When I hit 115 pounds, we both freaked. I went straight to the apartment and ate a peanut butter sandwich, which was mostly peanut butter, a half-pound of Havarti, a large bowl of ice cream, and a bag of potato chips. By eating every two hours, I managed to gain a pound back in the next week. Getting back to normal.

When David began to understand that I'd been alone, and what had happened to me while he was in the SICU, he was irate. He called Douglas Evans, explaining, and then protesting my isolation, demanding accountability. Our experience with Hopkins and the Mayo made us expect clear communication from our medical team. When David told Douglas Evans, the chair of the department, that the surgeon had not appeared for a week, Evans commented, "Craig had better have been at a conference." Ignoring a patient and spouse for a week during a death threatening event was/is not acceptable. Overhearing this telephone conversation brought on another flashback. These continued with increasing frequency and intensity for several weeks.

David was good with flashbacks; he knew just what to do. Holding me very tightly, he let me talk, even though I was speaking incoherently. David would press his forehead against mine, what he called a "mind meld," to absorb my trauma. Usually, it took not more than five minutes to get out of the flashback. But, at this time, they recurred often. By the July 3 fireworks, we were still going to bed before 8:00 p.m. I gave our apartment key to Mary Beth, who took her family to our balcony while we slept.

For the rest of the summer, for distraction, I looked out the windows at the intricate moving patterns of the boats. The bravest of the sailboats were ghostly and far from the breakwater. As it began to get dark, the sailboats came into the inner harbor for the night. The power boats stayed out until nearly 8:45 p.m., then they all scurried to dock before dark. From my perch, I watched the very large birds, which must have been gulls, soaring by swiftly and efficiently. Our peregrine falcon had deserted us in early spring, probably finding a building which furnished pigeons. A small house sparrow kept trying to find a place to nest on our cement balcony and roofline. He couldn't find purchase, yet he tried every night.

My mind was too cluttered with images to read, so when I wasn't looking out our windows, I listened to a book on tape: *George F. Kennan: An American Life* mesmerized me. To make it even more interesting, this very gifted diplomat was born and bred in Milwaukee. In 1947, Kennan authored the containment policy which attempted to stop Russia. I finished the first twenty hours of the thirty-eight-hour biography. Then, getting back some concentration, I was able to start reading a book of very short stories, about a page and a half each. *The Collected Stories of Lydia Davis* had a brilliant orange cover. By the end of the summer, the brilliant orange faded nearly to white as the book sat on our windowsill.

Gradually and slowly, we recovered, working towards remembering ourselves, who we had been. I had ignored myself, forgotten myself, had not exercised at all, nor slept well. My muscles were very tight from stress and adjusting to the machinery in David's SICU cubicle, and later his hospital rooms. I soon had a severe attack of piriformis syndrome, similar to sciatica except it lasts for months instead of days. I had had it before; the muscles had again forgotten how to work properly. I could not sit or stand, and could only walk within the apartment. During all our future medical meetings, I would lie on a gurney. If we went somewhere in our car, we would lower the backseats, and I would lie down in the back of the gray Honda Pilot. Not until February, 2017, was I able to sit long enough to fly. Clearly, I was gaining ground in the Golden Olympics competition for the most chronic illnesses.

As soon as the real, businesslike David returned, he requested all of his medical records, poring over them for days. While he never remembered anything from this time, the medical records frightened him. He marveled at their intricacy, but he was shocked by what had happened, by what had been done to him, by the intensity and complexity of his medical treatments. He realized his hospital stay involved millions of dollars. Earlier, he had said, "They saved my life," angry at me for criticizing the doctors. After he had fully recovered, he was infuriated, saying, "They almost killed me." He thought he remembered swimming in a seven-foot-deep pool of green water. He protested to me, "I was swimming. I was working very hard. I wasn't slogging off." On some level, he clearly knew he had struggled very hard to stay alive.

By early August, we were both recovering more quickly than we had hoped. David had slowly resumed playing Ping-Pong; by mid-August, he was playing forty-five-minute games. I was walking a half mile every day inside the building. Still not comfortable outside the retirement home, we were nevertheless beginning to feel some confidence. We had survived our biggest threat, our relationship intact. David was recovering; I pulled through the worst terror of my life, and we were starting to plan again. If we coordinated my breast cancer appointments with David's MRIs, could we go to our mountain home in Virginia between the tests?

On August 3, David drove our car from the garage to the parking lot, a big step. On September 19, he drove for the first time, taking me to my pulmonologist. She was amazed, scarcely believing how healthy he looked. As she and I talked about septicemia, I lay on a hospital bed. At this point, she was acting as my internist and was eager to fix my sitting problem. She ordered a CT scan, hoping to fix the piriformis muscle.

The next Monday, we met with David's medical oncologist, grasping the fragility of this reprieve and fearing that these quiet moments would end.

5

THE DEATH SENTENCE

By September 23, 2013, we both felt like ourselves, returned to normal, a new normal, but normal. We drove to the cancer center to get the results of the second MRI, a five-month checkup. We had asked a physician neighbor, a specialist in bloodwork, to accompany us. We hoped we might have two more good years so that we could go back to our mountain home.

I lay on a gurney flat out while we waited in the medical oncologist's office. His name was George. When he and Craig, the surgeon, eventually arrived, I asked about septicemia.

George went straight to the MRI report. We found the cancer had aggressively returned, two new lesions in five months. When George said, "chemo will not help, radiation will not help, surgery will not help," I bolted into a sitting position, grotesquely and surreally aware that the moment I had been dreading my entire life had just happened. For a minute, I didn't see or hear anything. Then, after a moment of shock, David turned to me and said, "How are you, Toots?"

George did not say, "You will die;" they never do. He said, "We will start chemo in two weeks." Why? He had just said chemo would not help. Even though there were four doctors in the room, including a fellow, there was no real plan. We walked around the chemo question for about forty-five minutes; then, our decision was made: no chemo. David would do another MRI in two and a half months, and we would then reassess. The prognosis was twelve to eighteen months.

We were unprepared for this death sentence. We had not been afraid of cancer, having always beaten it. But this time, not only had the cancer returned aggressively but the liver abscess had not closed. We had not beaten septicemia. We were not prepared for this worst of all possibilities—septicemia returning. We were again facing both cholangiocarcinoma and septicemia. The doctor left, and our physician neighbor said, factually and calmly, "You need a second opinion, immediately." We were grateful for his presence.

When we returned to the retirement home, I had to walk off the fear and frustration while David parked the car. The piriformis did not allow me to sit, but I could now walk a bit, and wandered in the main lobby. When a neighbor, Ruth, asked me how I was, I started keening, gutturally, unable to stop. The funereal lament seemed a response to the unthinkable, something not even imagined in our relationship. David had always beaten cancer, recovered well. Sitting and keening on a hassock in the hallway of the main lobby, I was aware of doors being shut and high heels skittering away. I'd broken a basic rule of the retirement home, grieving in public. Ruth took me to the privacy of her apartment and advised, "You need to see David through this. That is all you can do."

Quite soon, David called me. When I entered our apartment, he was standing in the kitchen, looking over the countertop at Lake Michigan. He looked as if he were facing a problem even he could not solve. Looking at me, he said factually, almost acerbically, "No more good times for us, Toots." Then, we were quiet.

We weren't thinking about twelve to eighteen months. We were thinking, "this could happen tomorrow." With the liver abscess open, the bile ducts themselves could become septic, and David would be dead the next day. David asked me what I thought; I said, "I think this one has your name on it." He ate something. I probably did too.

We barely slept that night. Sleeping a minute or so, then clinging to each other and hanging tight, then going back to sleep, grasping, sleeping, then grasping again throughout the night, aware that we would not have each other's bodies for much longer. The thought of being alone, not to smell his sweetness, his so familiar body, shocked me. I had already seen him die in the SICU, watched his dead body. Again? The image of the monster from Star Trek came back... but that was done. I repeated to myself: I was to die first. I'd been alone in the convent, not again, not abandoned again. David had never abandoned me. I had never even thought of taking care of a dying David. He was the one so good at living in the world and coping with life.

Early the next morning, David started looking for the best place to get a second opinion. Utilizing all his managerial and persuasive skills, he got an appointment at the Duchossois Center for Advanced Medicine at the University of Chicago two days later. We were both relieved, hoping that this renowned resource center would give us a reprieve.

Not knowing who else to call, David called Helen, who was also his friend. She agreed to drive with him. The three of us concurred that my piriformis syndrome would make me a hindrance rather than an asset on this trip. I gave David and Helen a tape recorder, which neither of them knew how to use, but Helen promised to conference on our cell phones. David and Helen stayed at the Drake Hotel in Chicago that night. David called in great excitement at being in a hotel again, and a very familiar one. We had not been in a hotel since we left for Milwaukee in 2011. He and Helen went to high tea at the hotel where a harp was being played. David was eager for me to visit Chicago again. He was so excited I had to persuade him to focus on tomorrow's cancer discussion. Back to business. I had been making lists of questions we needed to ask, and David and I went over the questions that evening.

The conference call went smoothly, but rather than the miracle we had hoped for, the diagnosis/prognosis was confirmed—but with twelve to fifteen months instead of twelve to eighteen. We hung up, and David and Helen returned to Milwaukee, having been gone little more than twenty-four hours.

As soon as the telephone call was over, I thought, David is getting the death he had been wanting for fifty years. I had fought his desire to die before and won. I couldn't fight this death; we just had to make choices regarding how he would die. Then, I started making a list of the roles David played for me; it was long. For all the ups and downs of our forty-six years, David was my best friend, my confidant, my coach, my best fan, my chauffeur, my medical advisor, my financial consultant, my adversary, my critic, and my only child. He may not have been the best at any of these, but he was the best that I'd had. There was no way I could fill those roles. I expected never to fill them again, and haven't.

Then I made a list of reasons for me to stay in Milwaukee after David died—few. All this went into a buffer zone to be considered later when my brother Tom called to tell me, "Give it up, Nancy. You've done enough." Tom had been anguished listening to my desperation when David had septicemia. He wanted me to take care of myself and to plan my future. I told him I had just one irrevocable commitment: to see David safely buried, as pain-free as possible, and feeling as safe as possible. I would do whatever it took to keep him from losing himself.

When David and Helen returned, Helen was surprised I was so calm. I had prepared carryout leftover burritos for lunch, and the three of us talked about our options. Helen left quite soon, and David and I faced the diagnosis. Intellectually, we skipped all the standard stages of grief: denial, anger, bargaining, depression. We went straight to acceptance, as we had with our previous cancers. We had been talking about death since we met, and this was our fourth cancer, with two pre- cancers, yet we had always fought them. This was an intellectual decision. Only with recurring incidents, and time, and doctors' visits did we realize that this death was actually going to happen.

We met with George again the next week, our chance to ask any questions. Preparing for our meeting, I walked up and down in our apartment hallway, thinking, trying to find a question which would give us the information we needed. At the meeting, I asked my carefully couched question, one requiring a yes-or-no answer: "If we start chemo next week, will David ever be as healthy as he is right now?" The answer was an unambivalent "no." Our decision was confirmed: no chemo.

It took a few days to quietly grieve, absorbing the emotional shock, the reality of the death sentence. Then we came quite quickly to specific decisions. Nearly a decade later, these decisions seem quite insignificant; we were not yet able to make the significant decisions. I wanted a new wedding ring to replace the original which had been stolen. The new ring would be for eternity, canceling out the "death do us part" clause of the earlier marriage contract. I wanted David to stay married to me after he had died. David got on that very quickly: three eternity rings were on my finger the next week.

David decided he wanted to leave me a letter. Since his certain death had no definite timeframe, he actually wrote a lot of letters, seventeen in all, putting them in one of his Southworth Private Stock Paper boxes, expecting me to find them when he died. Actually, he gave me these early letters about five months before he died; they are like office memos, recapping what happened during the previous week. They are helpful to me now, but his clarity of thought and structure would have helped me when he wrote them; they would have distracted me, perhaps blunting my own emotions. His last letters, rather than office memos, read like letters John of the Cross might have written to Teresa of Avila. He gave them to me as he wrote them.

Our more significant decision was to make something good come of our death. Chartering our own path to death, we wanted to make a difference, to break a trail for other couples facing death. David was in the business of helping other people make decisions, consulting with clients, connecting them to the right people, and answering difficult questions. It is what he did. So, it was not at all surprising that he was eager that our fairly unusual and very different skills, at least unusual in a married couple, be used in an attempt to create a document to help people understand the human experience of dying. We wanted to make dying an accepted part of the human experience, recognized as one of the humanities, perhaps the most important event in human life.

As a researcher/author, I had been journaling most of my life, dealing with reality by writing about it. It was my survival mechanism. During the most profound experience of my life, I did the same. During my thirty years as a full-time scholar, I interpreted documents. I searched for the most important documents and from that interpreted material, came to a judgment, a decision. I followed the same familiar process now. I needed an archive and created one. During the next months, I took notes, captured over five hundred images, and collected medical and personal correspondence, as well as a complete medical record. Most importantly, we recorded sixty of our conversations on my iPhone; toward the end, the recordings were not conversations but mainly the words of a dying man. The book project was a coping mechanism, as well as a distraction, a distancing. The project gave us a reason to live. I had begun the archive for this book.

* * *

EACH WEEK we counted how much more time we had, how many days: not enough. David's death kept being reinforced. Less than a month after the deadly diagnosis, we watched a Masterpiece Theatre detective story – we had been watching them for nearly forty-six years. We had not seen this one, "Endeavor," before and looked forward to a long string of detective stories. Then, at the ending of the hour, we realized that what we had watched was the cliffhanger for the next season. David's death meant that we would not see the next episode. Though David felt well at this point, death went to a different layer, deeper, more entrenched in our unconscious.

David refused to grieve, or did not know how to grieve, how to mourn the loss of our life; I grieved alone. The thought of David no longer existing seemed as unbearable as a monk losing his God, or a Jesuit losing his brothers. My identity depended on my relationship to David. The hole left by David was so deep I knew it could never be filled, and it hasn't been filled, nor do I expect it to be. I wrote to my friend Hans, one of the five young men I wrote about in *Infinity*, "The thought of David no longer existing in this world seems unbearable to me. I may be forced to believe in God."

Then I realized, forced or not, I did believe in God, but not the Catholic God. I was a monotheist, a transcendentalist, a spiritualist. I had always believed in the Creator—straight from my convent days, "*Veni Creator Spiritus*." I asked my Creator why he was taking David away from me. I heard, "He is ready. You have done a good job." Then I asked, "Why can't I go with him?" The answer: "You still have work to do." I thought to myself, "I have enough on my plate without getting hysterical and hearing voices, probably my unconscious." I decided never to talk to my Creator again and didn't for a very long time.

By mid-October, both of us desperately wanted to return to our mountain home. David checked on renting private planes, while I asked Mary Beth and Holger to go with us. We were terribly excited. Then we interviewed the local hospital; they were equipped for neither septicemia nor cholangiocarcinoma. In horror, we realized we were locked out of our home, trapped by medical circumstances in Milwaukee, Wisconsin. David's condition was so critical that we had to stay within ten minutes of the Milwaukee ER which had David's medical records. We could no longer even go to Chicago for a weekend. David would never have the pleasure of taking me back to the Drake, to Chicago, his childhood home, and our hometown of twenty years.

We decided to bring our most important mountain furnishings, mostly family antiques, to Milwaukee, making the coming long winter easier. I wanted to make this apartment feel more like a home. David worked at it energetically, finding the best movers in our part of Virginia and setting the date for the move. I worked with the people who were taking care of our home, specifying what to bring: a six-by-eight-foot engraving of all the generals of the Carthusian order, framed in wood from our own forest; the dining table of my great-grandparents; my childhood desk where I had pretended to be writing novels; a small table which David liked, and our favorite paintings, including "The Long Walk." We set the date: November 12.

We kept trying to keep a sense of who we were, working hard to hang on to our traditions. I think David started planning our Christmas sing-along in October. This tradition was essential to our identity. We were determined to have another sing-along, our twenty-fifth. David was laying out all the silver platters and songbooks when I suggested that we wait until November to rearrange the furniture. From the beginning, we had a sense of urgency. We had to do everything right away, or it would be too late. But by November, it was too late.

David picked up the phone on October 30. George told us that David needed to go to the ER immediately. The Liver Conference, all the doctors in the hospital who were concerned with the liver, had made this decision. I fumed in anger, frustration, and anxiety, but called Holger, my emergency driver, and David and I both went to the ER. David wheelchaired me and insisted they provide me with a gurney: the piriformis muscle was still in full control. David and I were in parallel gurneys. I certainly knew how cold ERs were, so I lay in my breast cancer hot pink "Fight like a girl" hoodie. That ER visit led to David's second surgery.

A few days later, George again called. Based on the results of the ER tests, he said that The Liver Conference had decided it was more dangerous to do nothing than to do another surgery. The bacteria which had caused septicemia was still in David's liver and if it went to the bile ducts themselves, he would be dead the next day. David agreed to the in-and-out surgery but adamantly refused inserting a drain. The drain, besides being uncomfortable, needed flushing every day. He said emphatically, over and over, "no, no, no." But, admittedly, we were increasingly worried about the risks of doing nothing, and, in a sense, we both were glad to be going into the hospital for an in-and-out surgery. As always, though, I feared that once in the hospital, he would never come home. I was always afraid that he would disappear again, forever. For the first time, I thought, "When will I start using the word 'I' instead of 'we'?"

David seemed frightened. I wondered if his fatigue and fear were partly the beginning of the cancer symptoms. How could I help? The fear that at the end I would not be able to help him overpowered me and started the tears all over again. I realized that it really would be impossible for me to live without him. I would feel totally alone in the universe, as I did in the convent, and in the SICU. Five days before the surgery, David was singing "You Are Not Alone" from the Mass of Christian Burial, and I cried because he was leaving. Terrible night. My whole body was restless and angry, angry at being helpless. David wrote soon after, his first letter to me, marked with the Carthusian cross, as in all later letters. He said, "For the first time I see some real likelihood that I can, with your help, make some amends for some of the past." He ended the letter, "Your support and love are the only human things important to me."

Our mountain furnishings arrived on November 12 while David was getting prepped for surgery. I realized again that by moving our favorite furnishings to the apartment, we were trying to create a real home for David's death. As the movers were unloading, I talked to David on the speakerphone. We were both excited, and the movers joined in our conversation. They all looked at Lake Michigan and went out on the balcony. They talked about the heavy engraving which took twelve men to hang. The engraving of the Carthusian generals, all of the priors from 1084 to 1913, challenged them. My brother Peter came to direct the hanging as he had when it was originally hung in Virginia. Peter and my sister-in-law Sandi helped unpack while David was in the hospital.

The surgery was the following day. The morning after the surgery, David called in so much pain that he had to hang up. During what should have been in-and-out surgery to insert a new drain, his lung had been pierced and collapsed, causing extreme pain. By the end of the day, he was taking two opioids, Oxycodone and OxyContin, drugged out of his mind, hallucinating and very confused. He told me not to come to see him: "Hospitals are terrible places at night" and "I don't want you in hospitals." He wanted to protect me from hospitals. After consulting my best advisors, I went anyway. He angrily asked, "Doesn't anyone do what I tell them to do?" Another drain had been inserted. Three nurses came to inject a third intravenous needle. It was unnerving to see him again not in control of the situation. He angrily told me to "get out," and I happily did laps in the hallway. He always regretted these outbursts of anger. Before I left the hospital, he quietly said to me, "Thank you for coming." He was in the hospital for eight days. I decided doctors were never going to do this to him again. Every time they did something, he became less David.

Lisa, the new head of the medical center, agreed to help me prevent another premature discharge. But when she got to the hospital, David had already discharged himself. He really hated hospitals. He arrived at our apartment on his own, staggering and drugged. He had probably called a cab. Lisa arrived shortly after, trying to persuade him to spend the night in the skilled care center. He sat stubbornly in a small wooden chair which had belonged to my great-grandparents. Lisa offered to let him try every single chair in the medical center and take his choice, but he simply sat there unmovable. He repeatedly and authoritatively said, "I like this chair." David was frightened and certainly did not want to go back to the medical center, but he was dangerously drugged, and unable to think. Lisa left, after instructing me to call the night nurse if I needed help.

About 11:00 p.m., I called the night nurse for advice: which would be more dangerous, to get David onto my flat sofa, where he could not get up, or to leave him in the chair where he could easily fall on his head? The night nurse thought I should get him on the sofa, and I did. Very early the next morning, David was frantic and furious that I did not get him out of bed, outraged that I had put him on the flat sofa. He was still on OxyContin and Oxycodone, still drugged. He tried to grab me to pull himself up. I backed away, I needed space. Frightened by his behavior, I moved away into the bedroom and tried to lock the door. I again called the night nurse. She came about 6:00 a.m. to get him up from the flat sofa, and, with the help of three aides, put him in a wheelchair and took him to skilled care. He soon called to tell me he was not getting proper food. His life depended on a no salt diet at this time, and since the medical center staff was unwilling to respect his diet, I arranged his release. He brought with him a flock of aides; he liked supervising a lot of aides.

The constant need to manage the aides kept me in a state of distraction and frustration. As quickly as I could, I cut down their number. There was simply no room for all of them in the apartment. The morning after the aides appeared, I woke with the mental image of consecutive and identical reflections of myself in a mirror. The images started moving to my left, one by one, until I was not in the mirror. I was nowhere. Disappeared. Afraid of completely losing myself in David's death, I kept trying to write.

David was home, but still drugged and dangerous. I tried to call George's direct number, but he would not answer my phone call or respond to my messages. When David himself called him, I grabbed the phone and reported to his doctor. "What!" he said. "He still is on OxyContin and Oxycodone?" The medical center didn't call his oncologist, and David would have kept taking this double dose indefinitely.

David went off the drugs, and he gradually became himself

again, strong and sane, horrified he had been a danger to me. He was again in touch with our harsh reality. David sat at his desk as I cried unrestrainedly. He looked straight ahead and said with decision, sadness, and finality, "I can't fix this." David had always fixed everything. We were looking at this death straight on and knew what the outcome would be. At night, I would touch his chest with a firm hand, hoping to support him as he slept or dreamt.

The hospital stay had again been horrific. For the first time, David looked like a man who knew he was going to die. His expression was grim and stoic, nothing Irish about it. In early December, he sat in the striped chair by the piano all day and didn't look at anything or say anything. That evening when we were going to bed, he said factually, "I'm going to die."

Dying is a full-time job, and I doubt if I ever attended more meetings. Things were always urgent. This became the nature of our lives; by this time, doctors controlled our lives. We were at their mercy; we were no longer free. After David had recovered sufficiently from the second surgery, we met with the head of the liver department in mid-December. For seventeen years, David had suffered from a liver disease called hemochromatosis. We thought of it as only a nuisance; he had to have regular therapeutic phlebotomies to decrease the iron in his blood. As a result, his veins were shot. The liver doctor was extremely concerned about this disease; we had not known hemochromatosis could be fatal. The doctor had eliminated nearly all salt from our diet. We had been eating less than one teaspoon of salt a day, and David loved shrimp, which is very high in salt. He asked the doctor if he could eat two or three shrimp at the Christmas dinner. The doctor said, "Mr. Maguire, eat shrimp." The cancer would kill him before hemochromatosis. But, even if he didn't die from cancer, the hemochromatosis would kill him in a few years.

The liver doctor didn't say anything else which surprised

me, merely confirmed what I thought. David, always more optimistic than myself, was hit hard with this reality. On the possibility of radiation, I pushed the doctor with, "Well, if there were a 50/50 chance for a cure, it might make sense." I knew David would die, but I had not yet given up the irrational hope that he could live longer. The liver doctor suppressed laughing out loud, but said, "You will never get anyone to give you those odds." My own estimate had been perhaps a five percent chance for a cure. Yet having the words said by a scientist made things factual. The doctor said, "David can drive now, but he probably won't be able to in six months." We thought we probably had four to six months of near quality time. David went back to eating junk food.

Trudging through this insatiable, messy, unresolved dying, I needed to talk, I have always needed to talk. But, aside from David, there was no one I could openly talk to at the retirement home. And David would not be available for talk much longer. I didn't even have an internist, certainly not one I trusted, much less a therapist. Residents might drive me to the hospital, but but we never talked about anything personal, nothing like what I would consider a friend, a confidant, except for Mary Beth and Nici, and later Iris.

Since I had no friends physically present, I chose seven of my most trusted friends, those who had been with me through major life events, from around the world, from different times of my life. I started emailing them a journal, "The Death of a Couple." In this journal I freely talked about my own fatigue, fears, disquiet, and confusions. I noted the changes in our relationship as dying changed not only who we were, but most of all who we were becoming.

This group responded immediately to my angst: images, poems, biblical quotations, letters, and even a physical book. These friends became my internet support group, the only place I could freely talk. One member of this support group, Ressa from Boston, a very good friend, came to see us over the New Year's holiday.

Ressa was working at the Folger Shakespeare Library when I met him. He was so bright and personable that I introduced him to David, thinking he might be able to help Ressa find a job with more advancement possibilities. Ressa did not need help, but we became friends and he continued to be part of our life. We called him "our adopted son." On December 30, dressed in my red "Klein's Super Thrift" apron, Ressa fixed us a real Italian dinner—with chocolate cake. David asked Ressa to be with me at the end and then to take me on a short vacation after the funeral. The three of us talked about the funeral, and what to do with me afterward. I was too tired, tired of the constant uncertainty, to care about anything.

On New Year's Eve, we met with our first hospice representative. We went through our apartment while we made decisions about where to put David's deathbed. It felt as if we were working with an interior decorator. I was concerned that David's bed would give him a good view; David was concerned that his deathbed not intrude on my office space. It was awful, terrifying, unbearably real. Too much. I remembered that my grandmother had died at home, but she had six daughters and four of them took care of her. I am just one person. I had been the hospice helper for David's mother, but I just visited her regularly, checking on her. David was insisting I have at least two hours a day for myself. He was worried about me.

Fortunately, after the hospice nurse's visit, Lisa came. She agreed that a hospice interview is a terrifying thing. We went on to discuss David's second surgery, which had stunned us all. The in-and-out surgery turned into eight days in the hospital, with David dangerously drugged for over a week. What happened? Changing the subject, I optimistically concluded that we had made good use of our time, but I frequently broke down, in anguish and fear at the thought of watching David die again.

The wait was getting harder and harder for both of us. David wondered what I would do after I finished my job as his death partner. Amazingly, but characteristically, the conversation ended with both of us laughing and telling stories. We both sounded as if nothing at all had happened, was going to happen.

Then David suggested that, after he is dead, I hire a private plane and go to the mountains with Ressa. And stay there until I wanted to come back. Yes, good plan, but what about widow work: figuring out how to pay the 24/7 nurses, writing handwritten thank-you-notes to people, and months of paperwork, changing credit cards and bank accounts, getting Social Security, all while living in deep grief...

Since David never went to parties, Ressa took me to the New Year's Eve party at the retirement home. Even though I wore a cropped red jacket heavy with embroidered jewels and looked cute, the event frightened and repulsed me. I did not want to get old trying to look young, acting young. Besides, I had never been to a New Year's Eve party

I scarcely knew Mary from New York, a colleague of David's, but she again emailed me on this day, "To let you know I'm here if you want to share the challenges of being the chief support for David in these last months." I found it hard to believe; I had only met her twice, very casually. I responded, "Your email was amazing, shocking.... No one seems to know that the partner of a dying man has an exhausting job." I doubted she meant it, but she did. She stayed with me throughout David's death and beyond, telephoning, emailing, texting, and advising. I counted on her advice. She had stayed with her dying husband for six months. She understood. I wrote to Mary, "I feel tired most of the time, but the hospice social worker thinks I'm doing amazingly well." I continued, "I find it very difficult to think of life in Milwaukee without him. I would love to talk to you." And I did, throughout the next five months.

After Ressa left, a few days later, I tried to get back into my usual rhythm. But David's discussion with Ressa about being with me at the end had reinforced his death; we were actually planning for it. I went to do my laps, walking the ten floors of the North Tower, feeling as if I were standing on a cliff, knowing I had to jump off at any minute. I said to myself repeatedly, "I can't do this." I felt like retching. On January 5, David wrote, "I wish you didn't have to take this ride, but I need you to be along and hard to explain why. I think it is simply that we lived our life together." The lake was steaming, preparing for a total freeze.

By January 12, David had sufficiently recovered so he could enjoy, as well as get through, a Christmas sing-along. We turned it into a birthday party for me—as the first one, twenty-five years earlier, had been. Still strong enough, David was in good voice and could lead the singing; a very fine accompanist, a resident, played our forty-year-old piano. About twenty neighbors attended, one had a very good voice. I tried to sing, but cried as much as I sang. We did it all, with the figgy pudding and champagne in our silver goblets. I wore my red plaid sequined jacket, which had always made me the star of a party. David felt very good about the party. He wrote to me, "The party was terrific, and it was good to see you with some bounce, being your old self." I wondered why I carefully packed away the Christmas tree ornaments, as if there would be another Christmas.

I was slowly learning that in the death pattern there is no return—we no longer made lists of happy times; we would never again look at our scrapbooks. That time had passed. The Drake no longer had meaning for us, nor did visiting our mountain home. We were too deep in death to do things for the last time. David would be missing in every exchange of human life. I became aware that for the rest of my life, I would never get a kiss, a pat on the butt, a hand gripping mine in the night, or someone to tuck in and kiss before sleep. I would never smell his shaving lotion or see the toilet seat up. I would miss his constant grumbling.

Beneath all this was the knowledge that on January 23 we would get the results of David's third MRI. Perhaps the lesions had not grown; perhaps the threat of septicemia had gone; perhaps there was another option. We did not want to separate, and we still hung on to any irrational hope. Lake Michigan had completely frozen over, nothing moved, and the ice clumped together like sludge. No movement.

On January 23, we learned the liver abscess had finally closed. I was ecstatically happy: septicemia was finished. But the cancer lesions were still there, not radically larger but slowly growing. The surgeon was unwilling to do surgery because the cancer was so close to the stomach. One of the doctors at the meeting suggested the possibility of a cure; radiation could be a possibility. David grabbed on to this thought and started interviewing and researching every major radiation center in North America. Hope. Our ex-monk friend Hans sent us a picture of the easterly cross, which is empty and has an opening upward—a sign.

6

DECISION

DAVID NOW WORKED HARDER on finding a cure than he had ever worked on anything in his entire life. Persistent on checking every possible resource, he called and interviewed every radiation center for liver cancer in North America. He researched in the morning while I tried to keep writing, looking out my windows at the lake's sludge, now ugly gray. We discussed the results at noon. We came up with one very significant issue: major radiation centers, such as the University of Massachusetts, would take David's case but insisted on the use of fiducials, metal markers placed around the cancer to help locate the site. Septicemia results from foreign bodies—such as the markers. Neither of us was willing to face septicemia again. In late January, David looked at me regretfully and gravely and again said, "I can't stop it, I can't fix this."

The odds were not with us, and we were both tired. David was weakened by his first bout with septicemia and by the second surgery. I still was suffering from piriformis syndrome and could not possibly travel. We waited, focusing on getting ready for the end. On February 6, while David chose his obituary picture, we continued to explore ways to postpone his death. We considered whether we might gain another two years by eliminating the two lesions that were there, before new ones appeared. Theoretically, we thought this might be possible. I continued to look at the sludge. By now, the lake had become so frozen that ice fishermen had built a temporary village in the harbor right beneath us. Life.

That evening, February 6, a telephone call from George, our medical oncologist, brought us up short. I had one major question. Would the cancer time clock be reset from scratch if we got rid of the current lesions? George said not only would there be no reset, but the day after radiation, we could be back where we were right now. Our last frail hope had been shot to pieces. From my point of view, the game was finished, and we had lost. I had an intense crying spasm which I thought might literally kill me.

We both thought we were at the end of the line, but David, grasping at any straw, not wanting to leave me, continued his research. After investigating every resource, he determined the best radiation center was in Toronto—the Princess Margaret Hospital, now the Princess Margaret Cancer Center. His early research suggested that they would do radiation without fiducials. We had a moment of hope. So, on the evening of February 28, 2014, we talked to their liver cancer radiologist. We found that Princess Margaret Hospital also used fiducials. The radiologist was extremely generous in giving us all the time we wanted. But, at the end of the long conversation, it was very clear there was perhaps a two percent chance of a cure, seventy percent chance of permanent damage to the stomach and esophagus, and maybe twenty to twenty-five percent chance of lengthening life.

We looked at each other. David said, "What do you think?" I thought undergoing radiation was irrational and would only cause more pain. David agreed, but insisted on taking responsibility for the decision. He did not want me to second-guess myself later. He stumbled toward bed like a boxer who'd been in the ring too long. The next morning, he wrote, "Intellectually things seem to be getting clearer. Emotionally more difficult.... My concern is that I will hold up my end and be so absorbed by my death that I will ignore your life." David had done his job and was as relaxed as he had been since the cancer surgery.

After the telephone conversation, I had an immediate sense of exhilaration: this prolonged death would have an end. I would be able to write again. I had the insane belief that the day after the funeral I would be back to writing. I would be able to finish the book I had been writing and rewriting for the last forty years, a book about cults, specifically convent cults. Finally, I had it under control; I had it right. I was extraordinarily naive. From being an intellectual exercise, even an acerbic exercise, David's inevitable death stopped being intellectual at all, and emotion took over. I was not able to write again until December 26, 2017, and it was January 2016 before I was able to read a book. The book which was so hot remains in clean draft form on my computer.

We had made our decision. There was no room for hope in any form, except the hope that David would die in his sleep. I am surprised we were able to function in the next weeks, faking it, going to a retirement home birthday party for David a day later, drinking a $600 bottle of wine, the gift from an old classmate of mine. In pictures of the event, we look cheerful; I even look happy in my gray-and-black sequined top. But I was knotted up with dread and despair. I was terrified of seeing him die again. Would I have another flashback? Would I have the spiritual and mental strength, or the physical capacity, to see us to the end? My mind endlessly processed what had happened, how it had happened. I wrote to my internet support group, "I feel as if my operating system has been removed, and I've not adjusted to the new system." I've never really adjusted to the darkness.

This decision changed everything. Although we both had known that David's cancer was fatal, we had a subliminal hope that some miracle would happen. After deliberately and logically choosing death, there was nothing. We had no more choices. We absorbed the irrefutable fact of our death slowly. David became more aware of the tumor in his liver, always on the alert for pain, waiting, never knowing when the pain would start, or how bad it would become. He was not sure that the hospice meds would control the pain. Most of the time, I felt like retching, trying to vomit out this reality. My emotions ricocheted back to the SICU. Would I see David shutting down again?

I did not expect to ever feel this kind of suffering, knowing that David would never leave me. What did we do wrong? The problem was we did everything right, and this was still where we ended. By March, my piriformis muscle began to relax, and I was walking more and more. But whether I was doing physical therapy, walking the halls, or standing in a group of people, my body seemed ready to pass out. David and I were jumping off a cliff with no safety net and no branches to grasp on the way down; the cliff was smooth. Echoing Samuel Beckett, we would say to each other, "We must go on. I can't go on. I will go on." I cried violently to myself, "I can't do this."

Looking at the pictures which I took of our twenty-six-month death vigil, I can't believe we made the decision to skip radiation, our last possible reprieve. Of course, we did not know what kind of death it would be—it was not as had been described: "You will stop eating and then you will sleep and not wake up." Not like that at all. The slowness of it, watching it again, now in slow motion, makes it all the more horrible. To have carried out that decision seems inhuman—to have been so relentlessly logical about it, like two computers working on an insolvable problem.

When people commented on how unusual our way of dying was, we would look at each other in amazement, saying, "I don't see how else we could've done it." Living with this chosen death was difficult, but it was our choice, and we were able to do it our way, immersing ourselves in the humanities. We needed all of them: philosophy, theology, literature, history, psychology.

For twenty-six months, David and I said to each other, "I think about death every minute of the day and night." We could not forget it. The depth of the bond between us overwhelmed me at times. The days were incredibly painful but also an unusual gift. We were able to examine our relationship, and as far as humanly possible, resolve it. After we made the decision, my brother Tom again tried to persuade me I would have a life after David died. I refused to even think about my life. I could not imagine continuing to live without David. I did not want to be left behind. I was committed to one thing, getting David safely in his grave.

But, like David, I slogged on.

Lisa was this year's chair of the ethics committee at the retirement home and asked us to talk to the group. Looking for feedback, we agreed to give a talk. By March 13, we no longer needed feedback but went ahead with the talk. David prepared a very careful draft of his talk, outlining who he could have been: a senator from Illinois, a priest, a prior, or even a cardinal. He proceeded to tell them who he was now. He explained that he had three resources to draw on as he faced death: me, the monastery, and his experience as a CEO. He thought his biggest handicap was his inability to feel emotion; he explained that I would have a double job, feeling for both of us. He mentioned that my family had absented themselves from his death and that we would need support from the retirement community. In reviewing his life, he gave himself good marks for his marriage and for his work, but he insisted that he needed an A in death, a solid A in dying. More than anything, David needed to excel. If he were going to die, he was going to do it spectacularly well. Perhaps his identity was already shifting to his monk self. He wanted to experience every aspect of death, as he later said to me, "to suck this sucker to the marrow." And we did.

I watched the faces of the fifteen people in attendance. Their eyes did not move from David's face. They seemed frightened, awed, mesmerized. When he finished, no one clapped or spoke, but neither did they want to leave. Finally, a bioethicist asked a question: "Isn't this just a new normal?" I found the question very dismissive. And perhaps attention seeking. Perhaps the bioethicist meant, "a new normal for you." After some minor discussion, David commented, "Normal and dying don't feel comfortable in the same sentence." No one else asked a question. Speaking to the group had taken so much of David's scarce energy, that it took him twelve days to recover.

Hard act to follow. Besides, I had been ambivalent about talking, I did not know who would be in the audience, and I was afraid of breaking down in tears. I expected indifference, a dismissive "Get over it" response. I had gotten that response three months earlier. I did talk, without a text, but clearly prepared, focusing on the need to build a community of compassion. I argued; if we are part of this community, we should expect support. I explicitly said, speaking of myself and David, "We are in trouble. We need help." Continuing to be explicit about this had little effect. My talk was not a success.

There were no questions, no response, no one was mesmerized or even interested. I started to feel invisible. I was there, silent, invisible, grief-stricken, and getting exhausted while David got a grade of A, maybe an A+.

After this talk, we knew that many people, maybe most people, knew that David was certainly going to die. Not knowing who knew was awkward. In hopes of simplifying and clarifying, we decided to make David's death as public as possible. Together and separately, we spread the word among the retirement community.

This public disclosure of David's death sentence created a problem for everyone. No one had yet died in the new South Tower, and, somehow, the residents seem to believe that if they lived in the new tower, worked out in the gym, swam in the pool, ate properly, watched their drinking, and didn't smoke, they would not die. David was relatively young, did not smoke or drink, and played Ping-Pong obsessively. If they believed David was going to die of this rare cancer, they would be admitting that death was possible for them, even plausible. They adamantly rejected the fact of David's death, as well as my grief. The attitude toward grief, as I perceived it, was that "mourning is weird, unbelievable, and in bad taste."

The publicity made our death even more inescapable, reinforced it. David would say, "This is real, the cancer is growing." We felt trapped, we were trapped, cancer had trapped us. When I woke in the morning, I would say to David, "I want to run," adding, "If I had a mother, I could go home." He would respond, "I want to run too." But we had nowhere to run, and both of us knew that I would never leave David.

Not until March 25, did I finally push myself to email our friends and family: "We have three to six months before the cancer symptoms manifest; at which point, we will call in hospice. Death occurs about six months later." Writing this email hit us harder than anything else, or anyone else. I never print anything until I'm sure it is true. This death prediction frightened us. We believed the prediction. I worked hard on focusing on the present moment, what the monks call *nunc*. On this day, a female peregrine falcon, a rather dowdy bird in contrast to the male, appeared on the railing of our balcony. She kept me company during the long spring. The harbor was finally open, and I could see empty slips.

After we made the decision, we both realized that nothing else was important. We could pause, free to pursue our new normal. We kept up our nightly conversations, keeping in touch about how to do this dying thing. We examined our day, caught up on news we hadn't shared, looked for more resources about dying. David was reading very widely, biography and theology. I really can't remember what I did. I took very few pictures at this time.

Exactly a month after our decision, we decided to take a vacation from death. David was still symptom-free; the two lesions on his liver were not affecting his general health. We drove to the American Club in Kohler, Wisconsin, about fifty miles away. I looked forward to a five-star hotel again. David carried the bags as always, and I followed him as always. Back to normal. Away from death. I relaxed, glad to be doing something familiar. David loved going to new restaurants and made a reservation for us in the famously intimate Immigrant Restaurant. It was terrific. David suited up and ordered his usual whitefish. I don't remember what I had, but I remember we split three desserts. David was at his very best with the waiters and very sensitive to the occasion, probably our last dinner in a five-star restaurant. He allowed the waiter to take our picture with his arm around me. I was wearing a multicolored jacket—mainly blocks of red, gray, and black.

I don't know what happened to David between dinner and the evening in our room. He had become increasingly uncomfortable, missing the in-house nurses, and the emergency cord.

We changed our room several times, looking for a quieter room. I was enjoying the familiarity of a hotel room and was totally relaxed. David sat in a corner of the dark hotel room, and said to me, almost in a monotone, "It's going to be very, very hard to leave you." I think this might have been the first time he realized he would be leaving me. All at once, he absorbed the changes in his life, the reality of his death; he realized he would never again go to a five-star restaurant, or anywhere else. It was too much all at once.

The next morning, David acted very atypically, very unlike David Maguire. He loved going out to breakfast, but he was upset at the all-you-can-eat buffet; he was rude to the waitress, so rude that I motioned her to keep away from us. She looked startled and scurried off. We left Kohler early. David complained about waiting for a bellhop to get our luggage, telling him angrily, "I can't wait for you, but come anyway." He chose not to wait and managed to carry the luggage to our 2006 Honda Pilot, and we silently drove home. That was our first and only attempt to take a break from death. When we returned, David said, "I will never leave the retirement home again." He had set his geographical boundaries.

In August 2019, Gene, a forty-year friend, who had worked with David for fifteen years, read an early draft of this book and was jolted, saddened, almost incredulous. Gene had known David as the epitome of independence, resourcefulness, and innate politeness, with an unfailing sense of appropriate social behavior. My description did not sound like David at all; and I had rarely seen David being impolite. Seeing David so out of character was a shock. Gene and I talked about my account of the Kohler trip, concluding that death is bigger than surface presentation. David never wavered in believing and trusting in his God; yet, death staggers the most spiritually committed. Toward the end of his life, David would say, "I don't think about God anymore. I don't think about anything."

After Kohler, our relationship shifted. I knew I had to be more aware of David's emotions, alert to them, to inconspicuously limit his expectations and decisions, and to be responsible for his life and death. David talked about going back to our mountain home, but I knew he could not manage a 750-mile trip, and I could not manage the intensity of his emotions. When we returned from Kohler, I consulted my wise friend Nici. She understood.

We had no path or plan: we had to make it up as we went along. Years later, I suspect there were things we could have done better. There were no preset markers, and we were continually jarred by the absence of discernible time. We did not have any idea of how long David would live. Since his health no longer mattered, we were doing unhealthy things. I didn't insist on the normal structures of our life. In a disconcerted, ambivalent way, I didn't protest when he ate junk food: bags of cheese curls, hot dogs, and Snickers bars. I no longer encouraged him to exercise, nor did I argue with him when he spoke over me, once saying, "I get to talk, I'm dying." What did it matter now? He was dying. I stopped sparring with him, became the undercover supervisor of his activities, and responsible for his health.

Realizing I needed a writing project to survive, I struggled with my piriformis problem and continued to take notes, pictures, and record conversations for this book. I watched the newly returned male peregrine falcon, large and hugely colorful, taking a rest on our balcony. I checked on what my ocean was doing, and listened to the ticking of my great-grandfather's clock. I continued to add to my collection of sunrise images. David kept up his usual schedule of phone calls and in-house meetings. In a sense, he continued his regular job, looking for residents in need, consulting with them, helping them resolve their problems. He kept up with the news and sports. A couple of times a week, he watched Secretariat winning the 1973 race

at Belmont on YouTube; if I were around, he would tell me, "There has to be a God. Secretariat is everything a horse can be."

When septicemia nearly killed David, I had decided that I would dedicate myself to making sure that no one in this retirement home would ever again be alone in a crisis. In mid-March, we called a gathering of the new chaplain and trusted friends and staff; we wanted to create a culture of compassion. Instead of starting a grassroots compassion initiative, what started was a committee—a committee discussing the nature of compassion. The committee became very large, then had lots of subcommittees. The committees talked, drank punch, and ate cookies. No one showed much interest in practicing compassion.

I became increasingly angry. I felt like a pariah, alone and disregarded. In this place, no one grieved but me; and grieving was unacceptable. I was afraid to get on the elevator, not knowing who might be there, or what they might say. I was terrified of the residents. Their lack of empathy shamed me, caused me intense pain. How do I respond to their queries? Eventually, I created some safe responses, such as, "Is that a rhetorical question, or do you want to know the truth?" When someone did want to know the truth, I would tell them, and they would hug me. Terrific. I needed all the hugs that were offered.

One day that spring, I was walking laps in the lobby. A stranger, a woman, was advising an elderly friend of mine that she was doing too much exercise. I injected myself into the discussion; I thought she was doing just the right amount of exercise. The woman stranger followed me to the cafeteria. Actually, she had recognized me from the author photo in *An Infinity of Little Hours* and wanted to ask me about my book. I did not know who she was; I certainly did not know she was on the Board of Directors of the retirement home. To her question about how I was, I told her; "The people in this retirement home are emotionally retarded." I followed up with, "I would rather be anywhere on earth than here." I concluded, "I hate this place."

By the time I went upstairs and told David about the incident, the woman had already informed the president. David was frantic about my comments, especially to someone on the Board of Directors. He was on very good terms with the president, and immediately called her to try to erase my words. David was very good at erasing my outbursts. But I had meant my words, and they spread quickly among the residents.

Three years later, in March 2017, I initiated a symposium about aging at the retirement home. David and I had given $50,000 to be used for the general good, and I chose this topic. I gave the welcome address and focused on meeting all the participants. During one break, this woman sat next to me. I introduced myself, and she said, " I know you." I immediately responded, "yes, I'd rather be anywhere on earth but here." She remembered and added, "but I see you are still here." When I accused the residents of being provincial, she corrected me and said, "they are not provincial, they are exclusionist." Then she talked briefly about what a fracas David and I had caused while he was dying. We seemed to have been the center of every conversation.

None of the residents seemed to understand grief or know what to say to a grieving person. I stayed in the apartment not knowing what rejection would meet me on the elevator. As I took the elevator to the twenty-first floor, with tears streaming down my face, a neighbor would cheerfully say as he exited, "Have a good day, Nancy." I think he meant to help, but he didn't understand grief. Others would say, "What's your problem? He's alive, isn't he?" The separation of death doesn't happen all at once. Separation occurs gradually, piece by piece, inch by inch, and I mourned every loss. Eventually, I created flyers explaining what words are supportive, which are destructive: "how are you doing today?" instead of "how are you?" The first question recognizes that I have an ongoing issue and gives more leeway in how to respond. Some people were glad to know, and tried the words out, uncomfortably, but that was all right. Most didn't. To quote Roz Chast, *"Can't We Talk About Something More Pleasant?"*

Throughout these fragmented months of 2014, David and I shared the constant anxiety of not knowing what was happening to his body, the marker on this one way trip. He was very slowly dying. He was learning to tolerate his body not being quite right, knowing it would continually be less right, struggling to live in a body that wanted to die. He kept trying to get physically comfortable in this body, trying different physical positions for comfort, stretching, moving around in bed, stretching out on the sofa. Clearly, something was not right, but there was nothing either of us could do about it. And he knew, and I knew, that he would never get better. His increasingly unfamiliar body faded continuously, nearly imperceptibly. I grieved every time he became less David.

We had lost any sense of normal time. Time simply didn't exist. Whole months disappeared, and days went by without our being aware of having lived them. We both felt that our time was unbearably short. We lived half-day by half-day, as intensely as we could, while always apprehensive of what might happen next. We had been on edge for over a year, realistically expecting the worst end-of-life scene we could imagine. Every night, we analyzed and evaluated, kept track of each other, and gave each other a reason to live.

On April 5, David wrote to me, "It's a day-by-day slog with the cancer. No pain. Just wait and try to help you get prepared. . . . Pace yourself. The final lap has begun, but it is lengthy." On April 11, he wanted me to record his reading of T. S. Eliot's "Prufrock," which had become a favorite. He felt pressure on his liver, wondering if this was the beginning of cancer symptoms. The following day, exactly a year after the first surgery, he analyzed where he was now in his death. He explained that we were waiting for the symptoms to start, but for a moment we could sit back, a pause point. David looked at himself as one of the dots in a surreal painting: he particularly liked Seurat's "A Sunday on the Grande Jatte" at the Art Institute in Chicago. He saw himself as one of the dots making up the image of God

David understood that the retirement home was filled with people in trouble, but nobody talked about it. He was choosing his spots on where to have an impact on the retirement home. On his seventy-seventh birthday, he had his first birthday party inviting all the single woman because "they never get invited to parties." He took out all the family silver and china and put on a splendid birthday party. All the single women celebrated David. He later created a very successful men's group. By May, however, he had to shut it down because he was afraid the Republicans and the Democrats would kill each other.

At this pause point, we were both relaxing and bracing at the same time. David told me, "You have no choice. You will survive because you are like a cork, and you will pop up as soon as what is pushing you down stops." We paced ourselves for whatever was coming, lengthy or not. We had not paced ourselves for a health crisis on my part. I thought I was catching a cold, but in a few days, I was barely able to walk to our adjoining bathroom. David brought me food and water all day, then called the nurse who insisted I go to the ER. I refused to go to the ER. The nurse offered no other help, so David drove me to the in-house doctor who had his official office outside the retirement home. Crossing the street, he put his arm around me and said, "You're my baby." The respiratory infection went on for weeks, moving me from one doctor to another. I was fighting off an increasing load of antibiotics the whole way. Finally, doing his last drive, David took me to a new clinic where a rhinologist proved I never had a respiratory infection. Yet one more sinus thing.

After this, David was absolutely determined to find a

support group that would take care of me when I was sick. We were both naive. In a retirement home, there are no support groups—everyone counts on institutional support. For the first time, we both felt dreadfully in need of help. For forty-seven years, we had depended on each other. No longer.

By April 25, we were finished with my non-respiratory infection. We hugged each other before we went to bed; David again said, "It's going to be so very hard to leave you." Two days later, David insisted I keep an eye doctor appointment instead of hosting yet one more compassion meeting. Waiting in the lobby of the eye doctor's office, I found it difficult to watch couples sitting together, wondering why on earth they weren't talking to each other, enjoying each other. I hated that David would probably not be with me again for a doctor's appointment. The doctor asked me how David was, and I said, "He is ready." She responded, "But you are not."

7

GETTING READY

AFTER MY BROTHER TOM, my trusted editor, read the previous chapter, "Decision," he wrote,

> It's a cold and in a word an ugly day. How fitting to read your chapter today. It's beautifully written but this reader's feeling is cold and ugly. But that is the obvious truth of death. There is nothing cheerful or uplifting about the process. As your life's goal, you are determined to simply tell the truth; this is truth in all caps. Overall, it's a powerful exploration of dying. Congrats on surviving.

That caught me up short. I started to think about it. For David, there was something "cheerful and uplifting" about dying. He actually preferred what he called the "two-year dying program" to an abrupt death. The lengthy death gave him a chance to reconnect with his colleagues and a few close friends. The two-year dying program allowed him to prepare for his death, which he had been anticipating for fifty-three years—since he had become a monk. He could help people without being responsible for them, without getting them another job. He didn't have to worry about his health, he didn't exercise, ate what he wanted to eat. He didn't have to worry about old age and who would take care of him. He had the "get out of jail free" card. He didn't have to worry about his future: he was looking forward to his life after death. Most of all, he knew he could simply let go.

I couldn't let go. David needed me to stay with him to the end. The "truth in all caps," that Tom referred to, was my own truth, the truth of the surviving partner, certainly about me. I had to worry about my health, prepare for an unknown future alone, and manage the emotions of both of us. I was the one who had to watch his death, die with him, be present at the funeral, then start from absolute scratch with a new identity. Where? Then, without David's help, I would have to figure out my own relationship to God. And, I had the job of writing this book.

With the attention a mother might pay to the marriage of her only daughter, I focused on the details of dying. As Shakespeare said, "readiness is all," especially in events like this. When David was in the SICU, I had realized that I knew absolutely nothing about how to bury David. I was all over the funeral.

David said he did not want any funeral. He wanted to be tossed into the ground, unembalmed, uncoffined, like a monk. I doubt if he really wanted that; David was a contrarian and usually said no before he said yes. I absolutely protested. "I need a ritual, I need to have people around me." He reluctantly agreed, with the proviso that his body not be embalmed. I could live with that. After much discussion, we decided on the cemetery in my hometown of Sun Prairie, Wisconsin, where generations of my family were buried. The Irish David would have to learn to get along with my family of Czechs.

We had negotiated the burial battle: David's body would not be dumped in the ground, but neither would it be embalmed. With that settled, we went straight to the Trappist website for a coffin. David wanted one "just like the Popes." We were both in huge admiration of Pope John Paul II, who had died very publicly and simply, and was buried in a very plain unvarnished coffin. I deviated just a bit in ordering the coffin, spending additional money for a coffin partially made of black walnut.

We went to the mat over the funeral liturgy. We needed a church. I called the pastor of the Sun Prairie Catholic church. I left a voicemail, giving, in profuse detail, all the connections my family had with the parish, including all my ancestors buried in the cemetery. The pastor called back, and David picked up the phone. By the time I got to the telephone, David was informing the pastor that the bishop of the Madison diocese was a total jerk. A friend from Montana, Gene, thought this bishop was very difficult, and his wife had asserted, "He is a jerk." I grabbed the phone, but it was too late. David had insulted the pastor, and not surprisingly, the pastor was not willing to go outside the liturgical dictates of his diocese. The pastor refused Gregorian chant, would not allow a eulogy, blackballed *Ode to Joy* for the recessional, and anything else David might want. Defeated. And I was a little irritated at wasting all my ancestors, and my time and energy, to have David blow them away. I still had to figure out where the Catholic funeral mass would be and find a priest to preside.

David focused on the funeral reception. He loved being a

good host. He went to see the chef at the University Club. While sampling every possible food, the two of them had great fun planning a funeral reception in October—a fall menu. David had wanted to die in Advent. When he didn't die then, he was frustrated and upset because he had to change the menu for the funeral reception.

In May, we visited the church of The Gesu, my church when I attended Marquette, two miles away. The Gesu was still as beautiful as it had been in my student days, and the pipe organ even better. David made an interior movie of his funeral, visualizing himself in the coffin and filling the pews with people he knew would be there. I put myself in the front row. It made this whole experience very real. David was happy to have his funeral at The Gesu, an appropriate place, I thought. He loved the organ and started planning the funeral liturgy.

The Gesu liturgist was dedicated to the standard liturgy, but David was a dedicated dying man. He argued until he got all the songs he wanted: "Keep Schubert out of this"; not "Ave Maria," I want Beethoven's *Ode to Joy*." Then, the eulogy. The bishop in the Milwaukee diocese did not allow eulogies, but with total and undisputable authority, David announced, "I only die once, and I want a eulogy." The liturgist hesitated, then said, "The bishop probably won't notice, but it can only be five minutes." That didn't stop David; he came back forcefully with a demand for a ten-minute eulogy. He got it. He didn't want a eulogy, I wanted the eulogy, and if I wanted it, he was certainly going to get it. All these jobs made us feel better, but they also persistently, unrelentingly, screamed that David was going to die.

By the middle of May, as we woke during the night, we kept grabbing hands. We suspected the cancer symptoms were starting, but tired and anxious as we were, we kept working the job list, a great distraction. David said to me, "We've got to get this right. We are halfway through."

We went shopping for a double tombstone at Rock of Ages. I was still sick with the pseudo-sinus infection, so David wheelchaired me to the tombstone store. We quickly rejected all the ready-made tombstones. I had a very simple and inexpensive idea in mind—two slabs of unadorned granite, positioned as two pages of a book. David loved the Wisconsin red granite. After hours of discussion with a very fine salesperson, my simple idea turned into a large slab of the best Wisconsin red granite. Forget about two slabs—the sculptor would carve two pages out of one huge, expensive slab. Then, the salesman suggested carving facsimile pages on either side of the slab so it would really look like a book. Immortalizing our basic forty-seven-year argument, we put one word on each page: on David's, "Rejoice," and on mine, "Truth." I also insisted on using my entire name, Nancy Klein Maguire, which upset the balance on the tombstone. The cheap Trappist coffin would be invisible under the very pricey tombstone. We were amused. Since David was hoping for a fall funeral, we were also worried about whether this monumental tombstone would be ready in time.

Our long-range planning was in place. We relaxed for a few minutes, and then looked at the more painful, but more immediate, question of David's death place. From the very beginning, more so in January when we had met with a hospice representative, David and I were determined that he die at home, in our apartment. David would say, "If we both want it, we can make it happen." I couldn't tolerate the thought of his dying alone in some sort of institution, and David clearly wanted to die in our apartment.

Very early, right after the September 23, 2013, diagnosis, while my doctor injected my piriformis muscle, David went straight to the palliative care center at the hospital. He started talking and arguing with a nurse practitioner. David liked her. Her name was Elizabeth, and she later became the core of our death team. Relying on her advice, we started interviewing individual hospice agencies and nurses.

Although we had spoken to our first hospice representative on December 31, 2013, the first actual interview happened in May of the next year. I had asked another woman with recent hospice experience to be at the meeting. Oddly, this hospice nurse was dressed in red velvet and, at our first meeting, interviewed David exhaustively, and, I thought, without respect. Her interview, not a medical exam, was physically so far-reaching and extensive that David thought she might be a veterinarian. I thought she lacked sensitivity, totally ignoring me as I sat at the end of the table, terrified of her and the "comfort kit." The hospice comfort kit includes morphine, Haldol, lorazepam, and other medications. We eventually had two hospice comfort kits in our apartment. Illegal, probably.

As the hospice nurse described the end of life in great detail, I decisively commented to the group, "We've got to get David dead, fast." David laughed and said, "You all heard that!" But David seemed to like her, so I decided I simply would have to put up with a veterinarian taking care of David. He finally asked, "How do you like her?" I hedged for a moment, then gave him my impression of this very physical hospice nurse: "She is grotesque."

The second hospice nurse seemed too young, inexperienced. We met with yet a third hospice nurse a month later, better than the other two, and we decided she could, possibly, work with us. I suspected that I would be the one administering the morphine when the time came. I found that my revulsion about giving David morphine had gradually changed. It is a pain pill. But the morphine in our refrigerator and the weekly visits from the hospice nurse still freaked me out. I almost never talked to the hospice nurse, but she checked David's vitals and took notes, perhaps a required task. Very fortunately for me, this hospice nurse came equipped with a social worker who was a huge help to me. His name was Eric.

Time was running out. David hated having his picture taken, but he knew I would want a picture of us together. A professional photographer who lived in the building generously spent an entire afternoon taking our photograph. David suited up and cheerfully posed for the entire afternoon. He was so tired that the photographer had to position him leaning against the doorframe. We were pleased and immediately framed the picture.

In the midst of these useful distractions, I found our emotional lives shifting so quickly that I had trouble tracking them. David had more difficulty tolerating me; he frequently silenced me and complained that I had interrupted him. He would say, "there's nothing worth talking about but death," but he was referring, not to death in general, but his own death. He was increasingly reverting to his monastic life. Carthusian monks focus on the "big event." Young men joined the Carthusians in order to get to God, to die. David's Carthusian experience was the most important time of his life; he cherished that identity. I understood all this, but I wished he didn't seem so happy about leaving me.

Death is relatively easy, it's dying that is hard, and by early July, we realized with clarity that the process had already started. I wrote to my internet support group: "David cannot walk outside of the apartment, now needs a wheelchair to leave the apartment, his liver is visibly enlarged, and he is beginning to be short of breath. He had been taking steroids for energy, but they kept him from sleeping, so today we are trying one half of Ritalin. The attending physician we saw yesterday estimates the funeral will be in less than six months."

Death seemed like a second skin that absorbed everything. I was frightened, not just for the loss of David, but the reality of the inevitable dying process. I realized he might have to be in skilled care at some point. I raged against the idea, but what could be a long decline and the faithlessness of my own health could make it inevitable. His increasing demands on my time and attention, as well as his demands for more outside help, made me wonder if we could pull it off. We discussed this a lot until the end of November. While he was still healthy enough to think clearly, he wrote a legal document: "If my presence with all the attendant medical support encroaches excessively, I would wish to be moved to the skilled care facility. I wish Nancy Klein Maguire alone, without any additional authority, to make this decision on my behalf." A lifesaver, for both of us.

My friend Mary Beth decided I needed a break. She made a reservation for both of us at the Pfister Hotel, the premier hotel in Milwaukee. I was ecstatic: out of here! When I told David about the plan, he was aghast and said with more emotion than I'd ever heard from him, "I can't be left alone." End of the Pfister Hotel. I think this was when David created the five-minute rule: I could never be more than five minutes away from him. This rule stuck. I understood that he needed my presence to feel safe, but I found the rule oppressive, emotionally abusive. The rule meant I could never be spontaneous, could never really get away from the retirement home, or what had become the death apartment. I felt, and was, trapped. Years later, I am still bracing for David's next demand, expecting it. Also bracing for the next rejection of my grief.

Increasingly aware that I would be the one to determine our legacy, I worked with our lawyer and proposed a grant for the Advancement of the Humanities in the Midwest. I started looking for the proper University, one that had the personnel to pull it off. A Marquette fundraiser for the Advance team, Betsy, had been taking me for "jail breaks" in the very few places five minutes away from the retirement home. Very enthusiastically, I talked about my humanities plan, eliminating Marquette because the new president was an engineer, not a Jesuit or humanities person.

Betsy told the new president about my plan, and he came to our apartment and talked to me for an hour and fourteen minutes. I did my usual thing of waving my arms around and being enthusiastic, and the president agreed to push forward a program for the Advancement of the Humanities at Marquette. In the fall, I interviewed faculty, looking for an initial planning group and wrote a proposal for the project. By then, I was having a lot of fun.

After our trip to Kohler, David had said he would never leave the retirement home again. But when a colleague of his organized a lunch in his honor in Northbrook, Illinois, at the colleague's home, he rescinded that decision. I questioned if David was able to make the trip, but he said emphatically that if he didn't go, he would regret it on his deathbed. He had reconsidered his previous decision. So, on June 6, we left in a black car, with our friend Lisa, the new head of the medical center, and our so-called comfort kit. Colleagues of David came from California, Arizona, North Carolina, New York, Washington, D.C., and all over the Midwest. They were David's family. David was at his very best, mixing with everyone and giving a talk at the end. He compared us, the first death in the group, to a "scouting party" on the wagon train. He emphasized how his acceptance of death and his sense of safety depended on me. He commented, "As you all already know, *Infinity* is Nancy's love letter to me."

We had started our expedition on April 12, 2013, and for the last year, we had scouted the terrain. David reported on our expedition and what we had glimpsed for the future. He saw two future problems: "How do Nancy and I work together?" And "How do I get ready to meet my maker?" The audience sat motionless and intensely focused. David was telling his family: "Let's look at this. How can you gain from greater clarity? It's not so difficult, you can handle it." Amazingly dry-eyed, twenty people sat transfixed. I had never seen David so relaxed and happy. This luncheon was David's last trip outside Milwaukee.

When we came back, David believed he was finished. Saying goodbye to his "family" was the last essential thing he wanted. He frequently said, "I'm finished," while generally remaining in good spirits. Shortly after we returned, we stood in the kitchen and held each other very tightly for a long silent time. We both were ready for it to be over. We did not say anything; we had exhausted words and emotions. They were also finished. But then, David said, "Maybe three more weeks. I could do a lot of good in three weeks." The human body, even David's body, does not want to die. The *tertium quid*, Latin for the third thing, which was neither of us, yet both of us, continued. Perhaps the *tertium quid* was our only reality, perhaps our closest contact to God.

David was harnessing the power of dying as well as anyone could—99.999 percentile. He had power. He wrote to clients who had been alienated from their business partners for years, asking them to reconcile. I would be surprised if his words had no effect. A few people from the death committee interviewed him; he answered any questions they had about his experience of dying. People listened. He spent much of his time writing letters to people, saying what he could not say in person. He used his energy to simplify our accounting systems to make it easier for me. He legally gave me his share of our mountain home, putting it in my name alone.

On some level, I seemed to have accepted David's death. After not sleeping through the night since the death sentence, I began to sleep, six to seven hours of uninterrupted sleep, and I generally got up when my alarm went off at 7:30 a.m. I no longer experienced anguished keening or outbursts of tears, yet in the middle of the night, I would wake and find tears on my face. The worst part of my day was my waking awareness that, relatively soon, David would never be by my side. David seemed eager to die, eager to get to God. In reality, leaving your body is an extremely difficult thing to do. A robust body does not want to die. It struggles to live.

David was becoming more aware of our separation. Earlier, in his Northbrook talk, he had said, "God has to fix this. I can't die happy when I know how anguished Nancy is." In July, as we were moving closer to death, he wrote, "I do know and am beginning to feel the extraordinary love you have had for me over the years. . . . Hard as it is for me who am not wired for natural intimacy to recognize." He reiterated his need for us to be together to the end. David always needed us to be together; perhaps because we were so intertwined, I was part of his identity. How could he die without his entire self? Or perhaps because he knew I would never leave him, always preferring him to myself.

Elizabeth and her palliative care team had just predicted that David's funeral would be in three to six months. That brought us to attention. We had not heard "three" before. So, David thought about everything we needed to do, and had done: obit written, tombstone purchased, funeral reception planned, liturgy chosen, pallbearers selected. I insisted we had done everything, planned everything, "you can relax." I emphasized, "there is nothing left to do." Then, he asked, "what about your funeral clothes?" He decided to again leave the retirement home for a very short trip.

David insisted that we shop for my funeral clothes, had to shop for funeral clothes. We had always enjoyed shopping for my clothes. My birthday is on January 12, sale time, and one year we went from store to store for ten days straight, only considering what was fifty percent off. We enjoyed the game. On July 10, we went to a trunk show. I had never heard of one, but we went. A salesperson from New York, selling clothes from the designer Lafayette 148, came with design samples for the next season and lots of fabrics.

Although now in a wheelchair, David supervised the selection of my funeral clothes, vetting each possibility, and taking charge of the entire enterprise. No one doubted that he was in charge. The salesclerk was not even second in command. The New York Lafayette 148 salesperson ran back and forth between David and endless rolls of fabric. I stood stoically, trying to stay calm, while the sales clerk draped fabric around me. Mary Beth crouched on the floor behind me, using stick pins to fashion the fabrics: a skirt, slacks, or whatever. At one point, I was enveloped by four layers of fabric. Fortunately, I had thought to wear a very thin silk tank top.

David critiqued: "No, that's the wrong color for her." "No, she will be allergic to that." "I don't like the different fabric texture in the jacket." After David had chosen two complete outfits, and was starting to work on the third outfit, I asked him, "Where do you think I'm going to wear all those clothes?" David firmly and emphatically responded, "I want you to have enough clothes for the rest of your life." At this point, the designer needed to know what size slacks I wore. I went into the dressing room to try on different sizes.

While in the dressing room, I heard David say in a stage whisper to the ever-growing audience, "These are for my funeral. But don't say anything to Nancy or she will cry." When I came out of the dressing room, everyone was looking at me, questioningly. So, I asked David, "What do you want me to wear to the funeral?" He looked confused and asked, "Why should I decide?" I paused a moment and then said, "It's *your* funeral." The entire store burst into raucous laughter.

We enjoyed it immensely. I thought, "What fun, what a marvelous day." But when we returned home, I realized that we would never go shopping for clothes again. Throughout the summer there were moments of reprieve, but death did not go away. I enjoyed looking at our balcony, which was vibrant with deep red geraniums and lots of herbs. Life kept pushing back.

The slips were full of boats and the harbor was dotted with sailboats.

David also kept pushing back, he was jerking everyone's death chain. He made a reservation at a very good restaurant, Lake Park Bistro, and when they asked what the occasion was, he said loudly, irritably, and with great energy, "I'm dying in two months." When he ordered a cake for our anniversary, he ordered it under the name, "Dying man's last wish." He enjoyed the dark humor. In late July, David wrote to me, "Things become very simple. How can I help you as long as I can?" On the evening of July 31, David felt his first sharp pains. My falcon appeared on the balcony.

In August, we worked on the eulogy. Gene, David's best friend from work, wrote it, but he wasn't able to read it because he, like me, was too emotionally involved. We chose someone else to read it. David edited it, and then asked me to proofread. Ron, a friend of David's, designed the liturgy program with intricate care and detail. David chose the image and text for his memory card. The prayers of intercession were my turf, and I asked various people to read them; my Jewish friend Nici agreed to pray for Pope Francis. We were ridiculously prepared for this funeral.

Knowing David was going to die was difficult, realizing this emotionally was more difficult, but watching it happen, inch by inch, seemed unbearable. A prolonged death is a labyrinth, with long plateaus, with no end in sight, not a straight line. Time didn't pass more or less quickly. We no longer existed in time—there was neither past nor future. We lived outside of time. I don't expect to ever return to time. Maybe I will become a real monk. I am going to treasure this outside-of-time. Perhaps God is in this outside-of-time.

I started to think about David's death as a separation, a painful separation, but not for that many years. I will join him and hopefully we will have stopped sparring by then. We will be the best of us, each of us being different but completely ourselves. The two of us will become one spirit and join a bigger spirit. David began to think that some part of him would remain with me. It may be irrational, but it felt right. I couldn't believe David's spirit would be extinguished, and perhaps he will think of me.

8

GLOSSOLALIA

ONE MORNING, David was sitting in his green leather chair by the window, looking out on the city and Lake Michigan. I was waking up; he began to talk to me. He talked slowly and seriously in a measured voice and a measured pace. I listened intently.

I heard every word he said very clearly, every syllable. But none of the words related to anything. Words were nicely grouped into sentences with a clear closure, but neither the syllables nor the word groupings related to anything of what we currently call reality. He talked for perhaps twenty-five minutes, calmly and steadily. When he finished, he got up from his green chair, walked to the door of the bedroom, turned to me, made a courteous bow, and said, "Thank you for listening to my garble."

I heard my great-grandfather's clock ticking, got up, and went to the living room. David was sitting in front of the fireplace. And he seemed to be perfectly all right, so I said nothing. When a few days later, I told David about this experience, he immediately said, "glossolalia." He explained that the Greek word meant "speaking in tongues," and he also explained that if he was speaking in tongues, he was probably going to be a saint —or close to it. He was being hyperbolic, besides pulling my chain.

When I told Eric, the hospice social worker, about the glossolalia experience, he asked me what I thought David's words meant. I answered without hesitation, choking the words out, I heard: "I do not want to die, I do not want to leave you, I love you." David had to say the words in the only way he could. He had earlier said, "it's going to be hard for me to leave you," but in a monotone, not with any emotion. The emotional subtext now came through in his astonishing use of glossolalia, his conscious body language, and his courteous bow; he thanked me for listening.

The onslaught of primitive emotions overwhelmed David. He did not know how to recognize the emotions, much less deal with them, except by his usual method of denial. David was a world-class denier. In many phases of his life, denial had worked well. He jealously guarded his defenses; in his words, "I worked hard for these defenses and I'm keeping them."

I was the human element in David's life, the source of emotion and spontaneity. He married me for my emotions, but, in part, I married him because he didn't have any emotions. He was my rock. I needed a rock-solid partner, somebody who was always stable, reliable, consistent. I told my friends that David was like a computer, dependable, logical, rational, without any emotional interface. I didn't ask for emotions from him, I had asked for stability and a space to safely express my own emotions. Now, I needed a response, an echo. He didn't how to do it. He had never done it, and I expected too much. In David's words, "I'm better with head work than emotional work, but what you need and what you will remember is physicality."

Seminaries and monasteries did not tolerate emotions; they simply were not acceptable. David's family didn't encourage emotions either. His grandmother died having her first child, David's mother Rosemary; his grandfather asked the nuns in the parish convent to raise the child. Being raised in the convent, did not give Rosemary any experience of family, and more than anything, Rosemary wanted a family. Ten years into her marriage, she became pregnant; after a cesarean section, she unhesitatingly named her child David, which means "gift of God." She hired Audrey, whom David called "Oji," to care for him. David's dad brought home his paycheck and gave it to Rosemary; he then played golf, smoked cigars, and read the newspaper. Rosemary did a very good job of taking care of the paycheck and was eager to be responsible for David. Until Rosemary died, she considered David a gift from God. She was very possessive of David. I was "the other woman."

David struggled with his mother's need to control him until she died, and beyond. He learned very early he always had to be in charge, to be in control. He could only count on himself; he had to know where he was going and how to get there. He learned this in first grade in Decatur, Illinois. When he started grade school, no one went with him for his first day of school. There were no school buses where he lived, and he had to change city buses three times. He frantically looked at the maps above the seats and managed to get there. But, he sometimes vomited. The people on the city buses were aghast and repelled. At lunchtime, while all the other children would unpack their lunches, David took his quarter, or perhaps fifty cents, and tried to buy a hamburger or something at the nearest store. The nuns had not taught Rosemary about children and parenting.

After the Maguires moved to Chicago, David went to Quigley Seminary. He excelled at academics, sports, and choir. Even as a freshman, he sang the solos in Holy Name Cathedral; he loved to sing, but, to the very end of his life, he was always terrified of doing solos. He couldn't make a mistake. He was everything his mother had wanted; David was her ticket to the upper classes.

David almost automatically went to St. Mary of the Lake Seminary in Mundelein, Illinois, forty miles away. This probably pleased his mother. In Catholic circles, the priesthood was a prestigious vocation. David's uncle was chancellor of the Chicago archdiocese; David could quite likely follow him, but David did not want to become a political priest, and he was definitely being groomed for that job, straight to the Cardinal's office. He again excelled, but after a few years he became so reclusive his teachers worried about him. He would go to the chapel by himself, awestruck by his belief that God did love him. God loved David. He decided he wanted to spend his time with God because he believed God was being neglected.

David left Mundelein after two years. David casually told his parents that he was joining a hermit order of monks, the Carthusians, in England. For his mother, this was a huge event. She was losing her son, disappointed, of course, that he would never be a bishop or cardinal, yet no one in the Chicago archdiocese had ever joined the Carthusians. In Catholic terms, this was as good as, if not better, than becoming a bishop or cardinal. He was a spiritual astronaut. A decade later, when I was teaching at Quigley, the faculty still revered him.

David left for the monastery the day after his twenty-third birthday. When he reached the end of the path leading to the Charterhouse, he was surprised at the size, shocked by the austerity of his cell. When the novice master took him to his cell and shut the door, David thought about the farewell party his family had given him, realizing he could not leave without losing face. He decided to stick it out for three months. After that, he planned to go on tour telling stories about the Charterhouse. By the time three months were over, however, he had found living in a cell interesting and sometimes satisfying. So, he stayed on, getting used to never having a night's sleep, wearing a hairshirt, never having any meat, and no cheese in the winter. For all of his ambivalence, he left abruptly after nearly five years. He was ecstatic to get out of the Charterhouse.

I met David barely fourteen months later. I did my best to teach him emotions, to humanize him, and I made progress, but I could not eradicate his family and the monastery. After not recognizing or coping with emotions for seventy-five years, the primitive emotions of dying became very difficult. I would explain what emotion he was having, he would listen, recognize it intellectually, and then feel better, more at ease. This became increasingly challenging as our death became more prolonged and more debilitating. David was living more intensely than he ever had before. So was I.

During these twenty-six months, David had a constant sense of urgency. He was frenetic for a while, not able to decide what was most important. Certain death gives great freedom, removing all sanctions, and he immediately tried to do everything he had ever wanted to do all at once. Finally, David was free to act out all the prohibitions of his childhood. He became the child he never had been. From being reticent and reserved, he became gregarious. He was on the telephone regularly, laughing and talking to former clients and old colleagues.

At times I would sense terror in David. In January, 2014, David described visceral terror, in his words, "the cold hand of death ... grabbed my bowels." He wrote to me the following day about "meeting my maker." He said he had talked to God using an informal "you." His last word in the letter was, "Wow." He was frightened. So was I. Perhaps this is similar to the terror which I feel when I realize how alone I am. No David. When I think of my own end, I sense the feelings David probably had when he was dying—facing the end of life on earth. How could I protect him?

A very heavy job. My own emotions were tearing me apart, and I had to try to figure out what he was feeling, what psychological place had he found? Where he was now? I had some experience in protecting people, I had been trained since childhood to take care of people, to keep them safe.

When I was five years old, my mother had three babies in one year, two of them twin girls, preemies. I became her right-hand helper, changing diapers and generally helping care for the babies. Six months after the second twin came home from the hospital, attempting to escape from these babies, my mother and I went to a family reunion in Columbus, a nearby Wisconsin town. Two aunts and an uncle drove with us. My world had returned to normal. Again, I was the center of attention, jumping up and down on the bump in the back seat. My mother told me to sit down, but Aunt Dorothy said, "Tony, let her be, she is so excited."

Moments later, a truck rammed into our car. I was catapulted through the windshield, landing in a nearby field. The four adults were unconscious. When help finally came, one of the aunts woke up and said, "A little girl was with us." The men found me in an adjacent cornfield. I remember shards of glass shattering around me, then nothing until I woke in the hospital the next morning. My dad came to see me, but the nuns would not let me see my mother, though I knew she was in the next room.

Someone, probably my dad, took me back home, and during the long summer, I wiped the dishes and tried to keep my mother's house perfect; she always wanted it perfect. If I kept the house perfect, she might come back. I don't remember seeing my dad at all that summer. I was at the bottom of the triage list, hurting, frightened, and silent. Not until mid-July, when our next-door neighbor, Uncle Eddie, threw me into the air and caught me, did I scream. Someone took me to our family doctor who found a broken collarbone. I spent the rest of the summer in an iron brace lined with itchy cotton.

My mother was in the hospital until late August. She had had a brain concussion. My dad, an entrepreneur without health insurance, frantically tried to find women to take care of the preemie twins and to pay the bills. Somehow, he managed to regularly visit my mother in a Madison hospital. Oddly, my mother's six sisters were not present, nor my grandmother. I don't remember going to the farm that summer. When my mother finally came home in late August, she had forgotten that I was her right-hand daughter. She forgot me. She no longer cared about me or the house; she rushed straight upstairs to see the twins, who had become the controlling element in our family.

At age six, I felt not only responsible for somehow reconstructing my world, but I also thought I was responsible for those damn babies. I clearly remember putting three baby bottles in the special very high pot while standing on a stool in a blue-and-white checkered dress. Worried that I might get the milk too hot and kill the babies, I carefully squeezed some of the milk on my wrist to test it, as my mother had done. I did not know where my mother was; for several years, she would often just disappear. She didn't seem able to concentrate, even on playing bridge, or to obsess about the perfection of the living room. She came back to life when I was in about third or fourth grade. The house again became important, as did bridge club and my piano lessons.

When I was fifteen, my dad had a major heart attack. I tried to protect him by promising God I would become a nun if he lived. After about three months, he was released from the hospital with a prognosis of one day, or perhaps ten years. I became accustomed to living with plausible death, with fear of death. I did not tell anyone about my promise to God, but the next summer I got an application to join a convent. I thought it was a bill from God. It wasn't.

My mother and two of her religious siblings, a nun and a priest, had arranged to send me to the Benedictines, the order of my nun-aunt. I did not plan to stay. I thought, maybe in a month or two, God would send me elsewhere to further my career as a concert pianist. Yet, once I was there, I could not find a way out. My dad wanted to take me home, but my mother insisted I had to learn to adjust, adding, "perhaps your father and I are not holy enough to have a daughter for a nun." I was trapped. This particular convent was abusive in many ways: identity theft, sexual abuse, social abuse, educational abuse... The abuse was introduced during the novitiate.

While novices folded laundry or did other domestic tasks under the supervision of the novice mistress, we were allowed to talk to each other, there were three of us. Among other things, we washed the nun's sanitary napkins, putting them in a huge pot of boiling water, stirring them with a long stick: the stench was gross. When they were clean, we put them in a rickety old dryer and folded them before putting them on the appropriate nun shelf. Each carefully hemmed sanitary napkin had the nuns name tag sewed onto it.

Every night, I had gone to bed hoping I would not wake up, but I believed the jail sentence kept my dad alive. I had learned that I could tolerate anything, and I could, until David became septic. By the time, I was twenty-three, my brain had significantly matured, and I left. I no longer believed in convents or promises to God.

My relationship with my mother was difficult, continued to be difficult. I always hoped for my mother's affirmation but never got it. No matter how well I did in school or in my piano competitions, she would say, "I did better." When I was in my early 40s, I asked her, "why did you never like me?" She told me angrily, "your father and I were heartbroken when you went to the convent. We planned to send you to Europe to study piano." She followed that by, "You even failed at being a nun." I didn't see her, talk to her, or write to her for several years after that conversation.

When she was in her nineties, she could no longer harm me, so in some inexplicable way, I reconciled with her. I called her frequently. On one phone call, she said, "my mother had twelve children, I only had six." I assured her that her children were very well-educated and told her the names of their degrees. She then asked, "what about Nancy?" I replied, "Nancy has a PhD." She responded, "Nancy's good for nothing. She never had any children." Oddly, I felt validated, my analysis had been correct.

So, I looked for validation from David, perhaps unreasonably. He always supported me professionally, but now, I needed his emotional affirmation. When I praised him for thanking everyone in the assisted living quarters, I wanted him to also thank me, but he said, "I will never thank you." He simply did not know how to give emotional validation. I needed a full body hug, a kiss that meant something. He knew what I needed, but he simply couldn't do it. For twenty-six months, he kept repeating the words, "I love you." Finally, he asked, with frustration and anger, "Have I said I love you often enough?"

We struggled to stay together, carrying out our death decision. Our routine practice of meeting every night for an hour or so of conversation seemed critical. Sometimes I turned on my iPhone recorder, not knowing what words would emerge; sometimes I didn't. What I captured on the recordings shows a vast emergence of attitudes and emotions. Some were very calm acceptance of our life, others were angry, and in others we argued about important things, such as: who was in charge, who was right, who was right first?

By early spring 2014, I had already realized that we could no longer be equal partners, codependent. Now, I had to stop being dependent on David in any way; he had become more and more dependent on me. If he were not in charge of the situation, he became anxious. To calm him, I acted as if he were always in control of his life and death. One morning in Fall, when I went into our bedroom, David was sitting in his favorite antique wooden chair, shaking with anxiety. All I could do was put my arms around him, saying, "I've got you. I've got you." Then, he would calm down. He would not admit to being anxious, but finally admitted to having the "wobblies." He said to me with great urgency, "You are my tranquilizer." He finally agreed to take tranquilizers, but until then, I was his tranquilizer. When I was with him, he felt safe. He had lost control of his body and his life and needed to control his death, and me. He frequently asked me, "How long do you want me to live?" I always said, "As long as we can communicate in any way."

From being very reserved, encased in kryptonite, allowing acquaintances to only know he had been a monk, he became open to the people around him. He talked about his life, his death; he talked even more about the monastery. But still, no one ever knew his feelings. I had been pushing toward intimacy for forty-seven years, and I pushed again. David responded, "I have revealed more of myself to you than to any other human being." I asked him who he wanted to be with him when he died. My question upset him, and he replied, "Who would I want but you? You are my life."

We managed to stay in relationship, with adjustments needing to be made at least every ten minutes. With great frustration and pain on both our parts, we had accepted the reality —David could no longer support me, perhaps his most difficult reality. For me, the difficulty was maintaining a relationship with a dying man obsessed with his own death. After feeling and interpreting David's emotions for forty-seven years, we were an emotional totality, a single unit. I always felt what he felt, even though he was frequently unaware of his emotions. We had fused into a third identity, the *tertium quid*.

I still feel the emotions that David would have experienced if he were alive. After David died, I kept trying to regain my identity; searching for something, any part, of Nancy Klein Maguire. Seven years later, I'm recognizing that I can never regain that identity. David was the essential part of my identity.

9

BIRTHING INTO DEATH

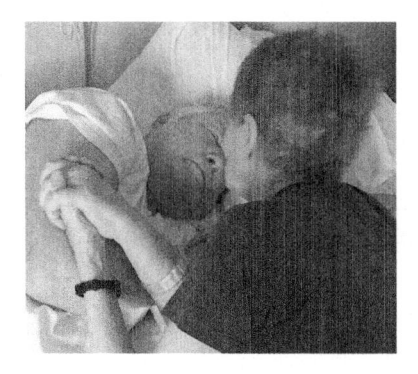

IN THE RETIREMENT HOME, we were living together, sharing office space, and we had never learned how to do that. We had lived parallel lives, which intersected only when we chose. We struggled. Who was in charge? I was taking care of David, but he was still there, asking, "Who is making the decisions? I am still in charge of me."

By mid-August, David's cancer had become more aggressive, his estimated lifespan moving toward three months. He was finding it harder to be in charge, and I was finding it harder to make him think that he was in charge. He was dying as well as anyone could, and I was doing my best to support him. It was difficult. He constantly made demands and expected everyone to give him what he wanted. They did. At the same time, David was becoming less and less the David I'd known. I asked my internet support group to send me energy, strength, whatever they had, to help me stay with David until the end.

We were prepared for the physical changes; we were not prepared for the mental losses: agility, impeccable judgment, delight in words and numbers. He regularly asked me to tell him if I noticed a change in his body or mind. He wanted to know exactly what was happening to him, and every time I found him less David, I reported the decline to him. Since April 2013, he had become accustomed to losses, but he still had to continually adapt to them, to recoup.

His continually shifting world was also wearing me out: adjusting to the changes in David, compensating for them, recalibrating my own identity. I was becoming increasingly fatigued, marginalized, and invisible. I seriously needed some contact with life. My only activity outside the retirement home was physical therapy. My therapist kept me alive. David tolerated my absence for physical therapy, but made sure I came straight home.

From being a relationship of mutual support, the relationship continued to move toward support for David. I could no longer count on David for support of any kind. My needs were pretty much off the table. About this time, Eric, our hospice social worker, told me two things: "David is no longer capable of thinking about you," and "You have to make the decisions from now on." David also recognized the change.

One morning, when I walked into our bedroom, he was quietly sitting in his antique armchair. As I entered the room and stood across from him, he looked at me and asked, "Can you take care of both of us?" I thought for a moment and said, "Yes I can." With that he was satisfied and settled into his thoughts. Some weeks later, he said to me, "I'm now a patient. I don't have to take care of myself, clean up after myself."

I desperately needed to get out of the apartment. The five-minute rule had stayed in place. That restriction hamstrung, depleted, and frustrated me, besides making me very irritable. I seriously needed a break. Elizabeth, the palliative care nurse practitioner, and Eric the hospice social worker, worked to get me a nine-minute rule, or even a seven-minute rule, but David was adamant about five. I was geographically trapped. David had trapped me.

As we moved closer to death, I realized I had to separate from David, sever our relationship, so that I could see us through to the end. I could no longer look to him for help. I could no longer spar with him; I had to be responsible for both of us. We were consciously separating. I tried to carve out some mornings to write. I watched my falcon on our balcony and listened to the dependable ticking of my great-grandfather's clock. I religiously walked every day and did my wimpy exercises. When I was walking, people might ask, "How are you?" I was always hurting, always fearful, always feeling vulnerable, often nauseous, and sometimes I felt like vomiting. I would usually say something generic, like "Okay" or "Hanging in." I controlled the conversation toward areas that would not bring on tears. In spite of all my efforts at detachment, death never left my consciousness. After receding momentarily with laughter, death slid right back.

On one of her routine August visits, I opened the door for Elizabeth and said, "Hi, Elizabeth." She walked straight to the living room, looked around, and said, "Something is terribly wrong here. Nancy is looking stressed and exhausted, and David is looking relaxed and having a good time." As I remember, David was having a lunch one of his friends had brought him. Elizabeth told David, "You are dying. You have cancer. You must be responsible for yourself." She added, "And if you want

Nancy with you at the end, you are going to have to give her a break." At Elizabeth's insistence, I got one. On August 22, David checked into the skilled care portion of the medical center; he made a detailed list of what he would need there, including Snickers bars. This time, he thoroughly enjoyed the change and the staff. "These people are great!"

So, I had what is known as respite care. David stayed in skilled care for three days, and I was absolutely free. No five-minute rule, no checking on David, the apartment to myself, I could do anything I wanted to do—that is, when I figured out what that was. David and I had a few good telephone conversations; Betsy, from Marquette University, took me to campus and to lunch, with lots of conversation. I was alive and real again for the first time since septicemia and cancer had returned last September. The death of a couple, however, is complicated. Although I thoroughly enjoyed my freedom, I spent nearly an entire day crying. I realized that without David, I would have no one to call when I was late coming back from PT, no one to share my pasta bowl, or forty-seven years of personal history, but I still kept negotiating for more respite care—David resisted.

Elizabeth had told David to do just one activity a week—he did six a day. He scheduled meetings: the administration, the residents, the chaplain, whoever. He became increasingly exhausted. Looking at his still body in bed, I would be terrified, wondering whether he would stop breathing entirely. I often felt like a mother with a newborn, totally absorbed in protecting my David. I argued that he had no right to frighten me; he replied, "I won't do it again. I had to test my limits to see what I could do." The testing didn't stop. David was determined to live.

For our entire marriage, David had said, over and over again, "Just you and me, baby." He thought we didn't need anyone else, and we hadn't up to this point. But now he would say to me, "We need others. The two of us and God are not enough." He needed a lot of people, and he had them. When he could no longer push his wheelchair, he hired an aide to wheel him around the building. Flash mobs surrounded him as he was wheeled around the lobby. He had become a myth, the man who was not afraid of death, who was teaching other people how to die. A rock star. Coming back totally exhausted, he would lie on our bed without moving, barely breathing. Panicked, I would wonder what to do. Should I call hospice? When things were the very worst, and I couldn't decide whether he was dead or not, I simply fell asleep. Feeling completely helpless and inadequate, I would say to David's God, "Into your hands I commend his spirit."

We were numb from waiting, the endless sequence of days, weeks, even years. David became even more absorbed in preparing for his death, he thought of nothing else, talked of nothing else. As he had feared, he forgot he had a wife. Carrying the emotional load, I was becoming more and more fatigued. We failed to see signposts; there were none. We were in eight-foot waves without a lifeboat. To survive, we had to create a lifeboat for ourselves. So, we did what we always did, we talked and analyzed the situation, continuing to record our conversations. Listening to them now, I'm struck by how deliberately and rationally we processed what was going on in our death. I cried, but the tears did not stop the flow of thought or the tough decision making.

In some way, these conversations anchored us, but they also gave us a goal. We were collecting data for this book. During the twenty-six months, I recorded sixty conversations, usually three to four a month. In September and October, we made twenty recordings, an index of our desperation and exhaustion. They are also an index of how much we needed each other for laughter, validation, connection, reassurance, and occasional sparring, our form of entertainment. By November, we were not able to make even one recording. There were no more conversations until David was already in assisted living, with a two-to-six-week prognosis.

The conversations have a huge emotional range. Upticks and downticks. Vile fights, acceptance, living in the half-day—we could not manage an entire day. David singing for me, discussions of where I would go when he died. We talked about what it meant to be widowed and the possibility of David dying in skilled care. A lot of discussion about our relationship. We probed its nature: we were always questioning, nuanced, and comfortable with ambiguity.

David wrote to me in early September, "Changes are coming, rapidly but subtly. We need to keep checking things and staying together." He ends: "We are a formidable twosome when we get our act together," adding, "Thanks for sticking with me."

We started recording additional conversations beginning on September 12. At my suggestion, we started by reviewing our history of cholangiocarcinoma for this book. Then, David announced, "Things have changed, there's been a shift," and adds, "I'm taking care of myself." He is announcing that he is no longer thinking about me at all. He is taking care that he gets whatever he needs. I accuse David of being "totally oblivious of my needs and incapable of even thinking about me." David responds, "Finally, I'm clearing the decks. I'm taking care of myself." He adds unequivocally, "I'm not doing anything to help from now on." Very frustrated and infuriated, I finally say, "I'm overloaded, and you should be thinking about me." The conversation ends with a very irate, raging attack on me for not rejoicing with him, my equally raging attack on his failure to mourn with me. No resolution. The conversation ends with a return to this book. David comments, "Your memory is very good. You'll get it right."

Ten days later, our conversation was very brief. Nothing happening. Flat time. David says with grim humor, "We can't make it happen." We had had a whole day together, simple stuff, an ordinary day, a good day. David is incredulous that it is now eighteen months since we started dying. He pointed out that the long slog was our new battle. We talked at equal length throughout. I naively asked, "Who will take your place?" When he gets ready to fix some hot dogs, I say, "I wish I could have some." But, I had a GI problem. He concludes factually, "You will get better, I'll get dead." Hot dogs.

Hot dogs are normal. David was looking for normal, so was I. We were accepting the inevitable. There was nothing we could do about the long slog. We laughed less; the conversations became more labored. We were frustrated, couldn't make things better, couldn't help each other. David continued to be optimistic, looking forward to the end of his life. He never faltered believing in his God, morphed into the prodigal son's father. I just ground on, trying to get to the end, trying to hold us together. I could not rejoice in his death; I preferred him dying to being dead.

Now, eighteen months after the diagnosis, David was still an outlier, but even outliers die eventually. We both again hoped he would die in his sleep. Death was coming toward us very slowly, too slowly for us to keep pace. We kept stumbling. We were deep in change. I no longer remembered who I had been, and David more and more wondered how much he should alter his behavior. He changed more than I would have believed. From being a deeply guarded reticent person, he became much more open to everyone, searching out and developing new relationships. One morning as we were waking, he leaned over and touched my hair, something he'd never done before. He was experimenting. I think he cherished his ability to change, to become someone he had not been before. He was living out all his possible lives, all the layers.

By September 26, David asked himself, "Who am I now that I am dying? Should I change who I have been for the last seventy-seven years? Should I let people know who I am?" He notes that after Helen had terminated our relationship because it was too emotional, it will be hard for me to trust anyone. Who would I trust? I decided I would be more closed to people. We talked about my survival skills. David kept falling asleep.

After a good week, at least in our terms, I noticed the hospice pamphlet describing the last days of life. The pamphlet was short, and I thought it would be a five-minute read before I went to bed. Reading it, I saw David's dying face. I started crying with terror and grief. Then, I recognized that it was not my vivid imagination at work; I was remembering what David had looked like when he was dying of septicemia. The same physical symptoms. I still touched David when I went to bed, but it was with less attachment, not to give or get strength. Just verifying that, yes, he is still here.

We entertained for the last time on October 3, a birthday party for one of David's colleagues. She was an ex-nun and a two-time widow, and I watched her very carefully; she seemed perfectly put together, blonde hair and a sexy dress. I wondered if she would be a friend to me; I hoped she would. We served an elaborate and delicious cake on our best china. It was terrific fun for me, and I wanted to have another birthday party. But even a two-hour social event fatigued David. He was getting more and more tired, although still clinging to getting what he wanted with fierce determination.

The following day, we are again talking about David's death place and my need for another break. Both our voices sound strong, but the conversation betrays two people hopelessly trying to get through an impossible situation, both needing outside help. I am calmly indignant. I insist that I am tired, confused, and terrified. David agrees, factually commenting, "You have never been more fractionated." I need a break, David doesn't accept that I need a break. He feels very much at rest, very satisfied with himself, and wants to be sure I arrange my life according to his calendar. I give up, I can't make my point. I point out that plans are irrelevant at this point. Whole conversation goes on and on and on.

We were both dying during those twenty-six months, but David was unaware that I was dying too. David had always tried to protect me. He could not tolerate my vulnerability when I put myself in dangerous positions outside his range of protection. Yet, during these twenty-six months, he showed little interest in protecting me. I became invisible, even to David. I disappeared, not by choice but through a combination of the retirement home culture that I never understood and David's demand for stage center. He thought about my life after he died, but until he actually died, he believed all my energy should be devoted to him. It was. His notes include a chart that showed the duties of the survivor and those of the one dying. The duties of the survivor were, at all times, to take care of the one dying, until the very end. Only then was the survivor to plan a life.

On October 1, Mary, a very casual acquaintance, sent me an email. She had been a colleague of David's in New York, and I had met her briefly at one of our book parties. This was the first time anyone had asked about me. I was amazed. Someone understood what it was like to be the partner of a dying man. She suggested, "Let's plan to talk when convenient and when you feel it would be supportive." I could scarcely believe it. I didn't believe it and responded with a courtesy reply.

More support came from the monks. On the feast of St. Bruno, October 6, our Carthusian friend Dom Leo, one of the five young men in *Infinity*, sent David a sermon about death he wrote especially for him. Neither David nor I understood Dom Leo's theologically dense sermon, but we appreciated his effort. Our ex-monk friend Hans commented, "The band of monks start surrounding." During these twenty-six months, the monks were always there by email, even by next-day email. I thought of the band of monks who surrounded a dying monk and thought,

"I need some monks. David will only have my puny spirit." Another of the five young men from *Infinity*, wrote to me, "God our Father is so grateful to you for being where you are and who you are. He sees much better than we see ourselves." He ended, "And believe it or not, the fact is the monks need you to witness loving in the flesh." I dreaded the decisions that, at some point, I would have to make.

Beatrice, my best friend from third grade, living in a Milwaukee suburb, was becoming increasingly worried about me. She insisted on taking me to her home and fixing lunch for me. David was irate, but I had to get away from the death apartment. It was exhilarating just to be driving in her car, away from the retirement home. When we got to her home, I called to check on David who was distressed at my absence. We returned immediately without lunch. When we returned, David was having a very fine lunch; he had persuaded Mary Beth to buy him exactly what he wanted from Whole Foods. Beatrice and I were not invited, and I probably had a nutrition bar for lunch.

A week later, October 13, we were again trying to make the best of our time, struggling to cohabit limited space. David didn't feel like talking, but insisted, "We have to keep talking every night." He observed, "Too bad you have physical therapy. It complicates things." David sounds very stressed and agitated. I'm insisting I need time in the morning; I need to get David's fleet of aides out of my office. I say, "I have to create a Folger in my office." Then I am saying, with considerable anger, "I need to get out of this apartment." David is trying to plan every minute of every day because he doesn't know what he will want to do next; he needs me to be on a very strict schedule. Then, he could pace himself by my schedule. He needs to be in control of his time and my time. I say, "Quit planning. I can't stand talking about it one more minute—stop."

I wrote to a friend, "He is now very weak, has not walked for months, we are waiting for the end. I am necessary to his life—

what does 'I love you' mean? At this point, unrestrained egotism?" My loneliness and anger, as I reread this, shocks me.

I had been David's death coach, death partner, for nineteen months. Some part of me thought that I could hang on to him and keep him from dying, but I knew that, no matter what I did, he was going to die. Despairing of keeping a life of my own, I stopped trying to write. Betsy and I were talking about my Marquette project, when David interrupted us and said, "Nancy always gives 110 percent to whatever she does. I will die in two months. I need 100 percent of Nancy." At David's insistence, I told Betsy that I could no longer work on our project. When I woke the next morning, I felt as if I had no life, and I didn't. From this time on, I simply tried to survive, keeping David as safe as I could.

Listening to a recording of our October 19 conversation, I am shocked at our bizarrely grim situation. I needed to be outside our apartment and still be within the five-minute rule. We are simply trying to find someone who would let me use their spare sofa to rest. I needed to get outside of the death apartment. In this conversation, I point out, "My body is tense as a board, my voice dead, on the verge of shakes, my hands shaking, too exhausted to even send an email to Ressa." I say to David, "I pay too much attention to you. I should be taking care of myself." Then say, "I'm beaten, on the verge of a breakdown. How can I ever come back from this? I never broke down like this before." He is so deep in his own death that he cannot understand me until I scream at him, "Go away."

In the next conversation, October 20, David argues vociferously that he would miss me more if I died first. Always, an argument. We talked for an hour. He wanted more recordings of my voice, more documents. I responded, "Then let me talk, don't keep silencing me." I point out, "I haven't heard my voice for a full year." David explains, "I'm full of myself because I have something to say. I could carry the *tertium quid* forward and create something." He was interested in aging and might have invested in an Institute for Aging. He insists that I will be able to write a book about our death. He sounds discouraged and tired, describing his body as jerky, gradually sinking down. He reflects, "Everything blurs into one." I sound defensive. I wish I could have been a cheerleader for his death, but I couldn't.

On October 21, we made four recordings. In the morning, atypically at 8 a.m., we continued last night's conversation. My voice is still dead and tired. I sound frightened, desperate: I repeat, "I've never gone down this far before, never been this completely depleted." David is philosophical and theological, energized and on top of everything. Totally confident about the outcome, he cheerfully explains to me, "You don't realize how totally dependent I am on you." I remembered his dependency when he was in the SICU. David still has not realized the depth of my exhaustion, and my inability to let him stay in the apartment until the end.

Toward the end of the conversation, I ask David to listen to me, and he does. I explain to him, "in order to get you safely to your grave, I have to separate from you before you die. I need to separate now so that at the end I will have the strength to birth you into death." David points out that traditionally the dying person separates from the living, but he is intrigued and impressed by the insight. The next morning, he woke with great energy and said, "You will birth me into death."

On that afternoon, two musicians from hospice, a pianist and violinist, came to sing with us. We had given them copies of our favorite show tunes organized in our red three-ring binders. David picked the songs. He chose all the songs that had been important to us, and those that he wanted to sing for me. And some that he just liked to sing. He flipped through the pages, and the rest of us followed him. He even was willing to solo some songs, including "I'm Getting Married in the Morning," which he sang at our wedding rehearsal dinner. When he became short of breath, we finished with, "The Party's Over," as we had done at all our sing-alongs. When I thanked him, he said, "They are all for you."

Later that afternoon, he soloed, "You'll Never Walk Alone," dedicating it to me. I told him, "This will help me through the hard times." Since David's death, I have listened to this recording hundreds of times, perhaps ten times a day right after his death. David was beginning to understand what my life would be like when he died, what I would need. Even amid the slog, there were moments when I believed that we could reach understanding, and finally resolve our very complicated relationship.

Our last recorded conversation on October 21 is very short, seventeen minutes. I start the conversation by crying so uncontrollably that I can barely speak. I'm trying to thank David for soloing "You'll Never Walk Alone." I want him to know how important it was to me. David is still cogent; I suggest that he is still learning basic emotional responses. He thinks that is possible and is pleased. He realizes he is gradually sinking down, time to stop fighting cancer. He comments, "We don't have much to say," then he continues to sing/hum his favorite songs. He was as relaxed as I had ever seen him. After a pause, I stop the conversation with, "He didn't hear me." He was no longer listening and has sunk so deeply down that he's unable to process anything.

Very fortunately, at this time, my brother Peter and his wife, Sandi, took me to an appointment with my oncologist in Madison. I was amazed and delighted at the way they talked to each other. No mention of death, no urgencies, just ordinary talk between a man and his wife. We stopped for lunch, and again, I was in normal life, having lunch at a familiar restaurant in Madison. After I saw my oncologist, Peter and Sandi drove me around our hometown, and we went to the cemetery to see our newly installed tombstone, which was only missing David's death date. We drove back to Milwaukee. As we got closer, my good feelings sunk by the minute.

When we got to the retirement home, Peter helped me out of the car and walked me to the door. I did not want to open it, sick with dread and misery. I'd been free and normal for almost an entire day. Peter said, "You have to do it," and walked me into the building. When I got to our apartment, I paused before I opened the door. "Shoulds" rushed toward me. David was depressed and despondent. I had arranged for people to be with him during the day, but he felt he was alone without me.

I was entering into what is called "caregivers' breakdown." Coming back from a day with my brother and sister-in-law, just entering into what had become "the death apartment" made me overwhelmingly depressed. I could not relax. David seemed a young child, overwhelmed with anxieties and needing me to always hover over him. I was putting all my energy into making him feel safe, never having time for myself. Every day, there was always something I had to do, talk to Lisa, meet with Eric, reassure David, get food in the apartment. The multiplicity of aides made me tense. I had to think about what they should do, what can they do? I had to get out of the apartment. Being gone for a day validated my need to get out.

On her regular October visit, Elizabeth told David he should get used to being tired. She wanted him to slow down, take naps. David said he had never taken a nap; she responded, "You've never been dying of cancer before." She took him off Ritalin. I was glad, as he was calmer, less agitated. She asked him, when he needed something, why he called me instead of her or the hospice nurse? The hospice nurse came usually once a week. From my perspective, hospice did very little until the crisis care nurses arrived the day before David died. I consulted and listened to Elizabeth. Both of us depended on her. Eric told me that since David only listened to me, there was no point for hospice to say anything.

Elizabeth then told me, "You have to stay out of this apartment as much as possible." She again told David that if he didn't give me some space, I would not be there at the end. I commented, "His self preservation instincts are so strong that he will never die." Elizabeth turned to me and said firmly, "He will die." She again insisted on another break for me. David went to skilled care which he called "scared living" or "the lockup." The aides, the hospice nurse, and Elizabeth went with him. The apartment was emptied, free of death. I relaxed, recouping for the next round.

David's decline was gradual through October, in November, the decline became steep. On November 4, our Jesuit friend Nicky administered the sacrament of the sick, giving David some closure and calm. Following this, Nicky said a private mass in our apartment, with my great-grandfather's clock ticking the whole time. I put a very small table in our living room, and Nicky cut a loaf of bread from Whole Foods into very small pieces, using just one very small piece. Two other women came, and we gathered around the table, in front of the piano, and looked at the lake, still ice free. This ceremony reassured me, and David said it gave him peace. Although very tired, David did the homily, resting his arm on mine. When I asked him why he gave the homily, he said, "I thought I was supposed to."

As David declined, friends and family gave me a break. Mary Beth and Iris, a new friend, took me to a Milwaukee pub, Beans and Barley, for dinner. I had been keeping my charge cards in a snack size baggie, and I spent five dollars to buy a Beans and Barley plastic zip bag. I was exhilarated by being outside, in the evening, doing something normal and natural. When I got back, David was just waking up, frightened at the prospect of being alone. Two days later, the telephone rang, and my brother Tom told me to look out the window. I could see him in a fairly large motorboat, in the freezing cold. He was fishing in my ocean and had just tossed back a great big brown trout. He came up to the apartment, peeled off eight to ten layers of multicolored clothes, and ate the leftover burritos from Beans and Barley. What a week! Friends and family both. A few days later, I told Marquette that I was not in a position to be involved in anything but David.

Ressa came and stayed for four days over Thanksgiving. He and I checked out The Gesu and went shopping at the local mall. I bought waterproof mascara and a purse for the funeral. The mall was exciting. Life, and lots and lots of people. Christmas decorations everywhere. David ordered Thanksgiving dinner from the University Club, and the three of us ate at our dining room table.

During this visit, David was very anxious and irritated by the arrangement of his meds. He insisted on doing them himself but got confused. Ressa spilled them all out on the dining room table and, under David's tutelage, started putting them back in the proper sections of David's pillboxes. They finally resolved the problem of the medication, but it was very clear that David could no longer do this kind of mental work.

After Thanksgiving, David's health continued to decline. The tumors grew relentlessly, increasing his girth. He was more short of breath, a few phone calls could wipe him out. He grasped whatever he could find to keep his balance, even falling off the toilet. I scheduled rehab physical therapists, who he rejected. He did not want physical therapy. To his annoyance, I put bumpers on the sharp corners in the apartment. I tried to stay physically distant for my safety.

He got up at three every morning, but slept a lot during the day, as expected with the progression of liver cancer. He began to have trouble focusing on the job at hand: figuring out how to find his cell phone, turn on the fireplace remote, or put on Depends, which he had just agreed to use. Sometimes he had trouble finding words, forming words, and did not remember incidents from day to day, or even within fifteen minutes. Our bed was now too far from the bathrooms: their floors were sticky with yellow urine. He was angry at me because I was unable to clean the floors, and angry that he could not do many things that he had previously done.

He became more demanding and verbally abusive: "Who are you talking to?" "Who's going to feed me?" He was frightened and hostile, particularly enraged at me. Actually, not angry at me, I was just an easy and safe target for all his anger and frustration. I was unable to cope with his increasing needs. Friends, particularly my nurse friends, worried for his safety and mine. Outside the apartment, he continued to insistently put on the front of the happily dying monk.

Every day, I realized how hard it was for David, but I wonder if he ever realized how hard it was for me. The David I knew appeared less and less often. Watching him deteriorate before me, emotionally and intellectually, was terrifying. I could not stop the process. More than anything, David wanted me to be with him at the end, which he called "crunch time." My commitment had been to see David safely buried. At the rate I myself was deteriorating, I would not make it to his burial.

For my own sanity, and to help resolve these always intense conflicts, I needed another adult mind in the apartment. David did not want a nurse. I insisted. We had to have a nurse. The hospice nurse was of no use in practical matters; I very rarely talked to her. Our friend Lisa could not find a reliable nurse; she suggested David try a room in assisted living which had a nurse during the day. A practical solution, but not an ideal place to die. David, intensely angry, said to me, "I would never put you into assisted living. I would take care of you, I would carry you in my arms." I knew he was right. He would have put all his energy into taking care of me until I died. I said to him, "We can't keep on going like this, can we?"

He agreed to try a room in assisted living, on the third floor, about a ten minute walk from our apartment. Before agreeing, he held a meeting in our apartment with the entire administrative staff of the retirement home. With our gas fireplace going, he negotiated with them, successfully, for total freedom in his room and the right to leave whenever he wanted. He also got a special price on the room, and whatever other perks he wanted. But, first, to my amazement, he decided to decorate his room. I thought, "What?" David had never been interested in interior decoration. With two of his buddies, he went to the room and rearranged it so that it looked like a monk's cell. The room was small with a window on one wall that looked out on a dumpster and a road where people walked their dogs. He was satisfied, willing to try it for a month, but with some ambivalence.

After double-checking that he would get every privilege he wanted, he went to assisted living on December 8. David had been going to die for twenty-one months. Now he was doing his last lap, making his last trip—he was going to the place he was going to die, his death room. He carefully chose what to take with him: one photograph of me, his wallet stuffed with fifty-dollar bills, his driver's license, and his car key—the one with the battery. Lots of underwear and socks, a sports jacket and slacks, one pair of shoes, and his favorite slippers. No computer. No books.

10

THE RELATIONSHIP, CLARITY

IN HIS JUNE 2014 talk to his colleagues in Northbrook, David insisted that the work he had left to do was to resolve our relationship and get ready to meet his maker. He said, "Nothing will come between us, anything that comes between us will have to go. Nothing will separate us." David seriously wanted there to be no emotional space between us. I thought to myself, "I've been doing everything I could to keep him as safe and comfortable as humanly possible. Shouldn't we have discussed this?"

The last five months, David did exactly that, making sure we weren't separated, while fighting for control all the way. We never succeeded in living together; how could we not struggle in dying together? The deep bond was always there, but so were the two of us, and we couldn't stop being who we were, and neither of us had our usual resources. I was depleted, torn apart by the 24/7 job of being responsible for David's short remaining life and long death. I was unable to be the Nancy he wanted and needed. He frequently said, "I miss Nancy." Somewhere between severe septicemia and "I'm dying, I get to talk," the Nancy he was missing had disappeared. He was looking for a mocking, resilient, troublemaking, and irreverent Nancy. I certainly was missing her too. But there was nothing I could do to reclaim her, and perhaps I never will. She was dying as quickly as David, but relentlessly hanging on to the mental and spiritual bond.

During these last months, David tried to resolve his conundrum: commitment to God or me. He decided to start by tackling me. He desperately wanted me to rejoice with him. He wanted our relationship resolved, whatever that might mean. He hated that I could not accept his view of life and death. While I knew I was his favorite human, that if he lived forever, he would never find a human he liked more, I still wanted something more, I still wanted reciprocal emotion. Even though I was consciously separating from him, I still could not stop hoping for an emotional connection. I needed to separate, but I also needed him to mourn the loss of me, of us, of our life. I wanted him to shed a tear, to mourn a little bit. But he was either unable or unwilling to give me that, to give me human intimacy, to give me reciprocal emotions. So, we staggered on, in anger and love, in grief and laughter.

In his room, #3307, David immediately set up his new business, operating as a CEO living in his monk cell. On December 8, he filled out his 2015 Day Timer, putting in all his passwords and identification numbers. He was a Luddite and refused to even consider letting me create an electronic address book for him. For the first time ever, he did not list all his phone numbers. He kept track of all of his appointments, even the days on which he would only have a shower or meet with the floor nurse.

He was continually on the phone or inviting people to visit in his cell. And, in a sense, he enjoyed himself. He was having fun with a room of his own, setting his own schedule, and having a lot of aides, nurses, and staff to supervise. He enjoyed all the activity, being in control. He had regular meetings with the president and vice president of the retirement home, teaching them how to manage the business, to improve the retirement home.

I was allotted a certain time to visit him. The staff called it "wife time." He told me, "I do not need you now, I will need you later." For a while, he did not want to talk to me. In his words, "I do not want you to be thinking about death. I want to keep you out of this." I can't believe he said that. What else had I thought about for the last twenty-one months? Did he ever talk about anything else? Did we ever talk about anything else? Did he ever think about me?

I was happy to be in exile. I knew he was safe, for a bit, and I had time to try to put myself back together. The apartment lost some of the stench of death, and I was getting a rest, even from the five-minute rule. But it was a harsh separation, like being cut apart with a blunt knife. I occasionally thought I saw David as I walked by his office, or thought I saw him getting up from bed. We both missed sleeping together. I missed the softness and smell of his body. His body always smelled sweet; when I said that, he was infuriated, but it was true. I put my arms around a pillow approximating his 250-pound bulk, but he seemed already gone, already dead. Since I knew I would be writing to him after he died, I started writing notes to him. He was not interested in my notes but was frantic to get the mail, which I had delivered to his room. He was still paying the bills and checking our finances, even selecting stocks.

After the first week, he realized we were having more time together, better discussions, and he thought this was a good arrangement, but he still talked about going back to the apartment. He had not yet decided where he wanted to die and kept his options open. He had not even decided if he was going to die. Emotions and the instinct to live could even overcome David. He kept thinking he might still live. He told me that we were in a neck-to-neck struggle about who would die first.

During this time, David realized he didn't have a crucifix. One of my priest uncles had given us one when we were married, but it was a delicate wood carving. David sent the chaplain to buy an appropriate cross for over his bed; he wanted a wooden cross with a very masculine corpus. I didn't pay much attention to the crucifix, but, after David's death when I was helpless with grief and exhaustion, David's strength reassured me when I touched the corpus. David's long and complicated death made me believe in the second person of the Trinity.

During wife time a few days later, he recited his entire day to me, starting with getting his medications at 6:00 a.m., breakfast at 6:30 a.m., shower at 7:00 a.m., and on through the day. When he finished, he said, "That was very helpful. Thank you for listening." I recognized the Carthusian schedule, their horarium, and he did too a few days later. The reality was clear: he would die a monk. God would always come first. Disturbingly, he signed his last notes to me, "Religious, married, and single." His ambivalence never ended.

Our last Christmas was in David's monk cell. We followed the new directive: "I report, you listen." He no longer would listen to me at all; my My job was to listen. He talked about his life as a dying monk, and at the end of the day, he read the chapter "Togetherness and Warmth" from *Infinity*, my monk book. When he read the sentence, "Dom Philip had thoroughly enjoyed the singing and the chocolates… but he hated the festivity, the togetherness, the unmonastic feelings that it had aroused," he stopped reading and said, "What a jerk." I thought to myself, "We are making progress." David recognizes that his emotional withholding in the Charterhouse made him a jerk. He is criticizing himself, becoming human. That ended the reading for Christmas day. I was certain that this was our best Christmas ever, never before had David been so transparent. After five hours of listening and entering into his irregular monk life, I walked back to our apartment and collapsed on the bed, totally exhausted.

On December 27, David left his room to meet three people for cider and donuts in the dining room, a few minutes away. At that time, he presented himself as the David I'd known for forty-seven years, urbane, charming, and charismatic. But, only a few days later, death had already sucked all the air out of his room. My David was missing, and I found his room stultifying. I couldn't stay there for very long at one time; I took walk breaks in the hallway so that I could breathe. He worried when I left. One day I said, lightly, "When I get back, prepare for twenty minutes of sheer delight." When I returned, he laughed and repeated, "sheer delight." It was good to again hear his infectious laugh.

Wife time became longer. He gave me the letters he had written to be read after he died. I doubt if I had time to even look at them. When I read them now, I wonder why he didn't give them to me as he wrote them. They all emphasize one thing, over and over again: "I want us to be together to the end. I need that." "I need you to be with me for whatever this is." We didn't know from minute to minute what "whatever this is" would be. But we both knew that I would be there to the very last minute. Often, he would say, "It is so good to have you here."

A few weeks later, he felt so good that he thought he might be getting better. His energy had returned, he slept less, he was interested in writing more letters, talking to more people. He would say, "I do not know what is happening because I've never died before." I had never before lost the most important thing in my world; I did not know how to do this either. David was perplexed because he was surrounded by nurses, but none of them were helping him get better. He knew rationally that he was going to die, but part of him couldn't quite accept his situation, especially since he felt fine. At times, he seemed deeply confused about what was happening to him. Quite often, he would expect that he would get better and come home, as he had so often before. He seemed so healthy that he was ambivalent about staying in #3307. About this time, while he was still cogent, I told our lawyer and tax person that if they needed anything to be signed, it should be done now.

I suggested that he come back to the apartment to see how he felt about assisted living. Our friend Ressa and I wheeled David back to our apartment on December 31, exactly a year after David had asked Ressa to help me. As we entered the apartment, he looked around and said, "Nice view." He struggled to move from his wheelchair to our sofa, and then was desperate to look at the files in his office. I was worried, afraid that, in the tightly packed room, he might fall on the sharp edges of the Steel Case file. Taking some financial folders out, he unsteadily made his way to the dining room table, totally engrossed in the papers, a familiar job.

David had asked to see his coffin. The undertaker arranged it, and we were ready to wheelchair him to the funeral home. But, David suddenly decided against it. So, Ressa and I thought the coffin lid would be a reasonable substitute. Ressa got the lid, unwrapped it from its blanket and showed it to David. He looked at it for a bit, then said, "That's not what I wanted at all. I wanted a plain coffin, just like the Pope's." I had ordered the cheapest wooden coffin on the market, a Trappist coffin, but it had polyurethane on it—the wood was finished. Then, David again looked around and said, "Nice view, but there's nothing for me here." We wheeled him back to #3307, and as soon as we opened the door, he said "Home."

I collapsed with relief. Our apartment reverting to the death apartment would have been lethal for me. I could almost relax, more than I had in twenty-two months; I took deep breaths and slept. My biweekly physical therapy continued, and I was getting stronger, and the staff at the clinic were a constant support. Mike, my physical therapist, was my best friend in Milwaukee; while at the clinic, I was free from talk of death, and the staff focused on my health and safety. It was an anchor in reality, the normal world still existed.

Two weeks later, on January 15, the palliative care team told David he had two to six weeks to live. He disagreed, saying, "I have work to do. A friend's husband is dying and she needs me." With tears spilling over my face, I said, "I have a husband who is dying too." Watching me, Elizabeth was nearly in tears herself. David said, "I will think about it." I was exhausted and strung out, but David decided rather quickly that still he needed to work on me. Once more, our relationship regained focus.

The new prognosis put pressure on both of us. We totally forgot about January 19, our forty-eighth anniversary. We faced the same old issues with more force, even greater urgency. The relationship, interacting and reacting for nearly half a century, was critical to both of us. Time was shorter than we had expected, we needed more time. We radically ejected friends and neighbors from his room; we had work to do. I needed David to recognize the intensity of my love, but my intensity frightened him. He said he wasn't good enough to reciprocate. I was looking for a real kiss, a hug, or a tight physical embrace, but not more words. We tried to get it right, to analyze this relationship, central to both of us. We tried to find peace.

With the new prognosis, the roller coaster moved more radically, more haphazardly, more unpredictably. Emotions always on edge, always extreme. David did not recognize his emotions, but they were there, and I had to figure them out. He tried over and over again to assure me that he loved me. He insisted he would do anything for me, give his life for me, even stay alive for me if he could. He had done that before. He was trying to make up for the lack of physicality, the scarcity of sex in our marriage. I assured him that I understood. It was all right.

Although the waiting seemed unendurable, we did not want it to end. I did not want him to die; neither did he. I could not stop him from dying, but I hoped to die with him. I was terrified watching his slow disintegration, my entire mental and spiritual world disappearing, the intact world in which I had been safe. I knew I would never feel safe again. He believed, "Even though I'm dying, even from here, I can offer you some protection." He was right. After he died, incidents occurred that would not have happened if he had been still dying.

About six months after David died, a resident whom I had trusted came to my apartment at 8 p.m., and groped me. I stopped him, then walked him out. As we were moving to the door, he put his hands on my breasts, and said, "how do you like this?" Six months later, when I was walking in the hall outside my apartment, I met four semi-drunk residents who mocked me, while laughing to themselves. I had never seen two of them. They started talking about David, making fun of him. I was again in shock.

I never knew what to expect when I entered David's cell, #3307, but I was never surprised to find David in control, or trying to control, the situation. Four days after the new prognosis, he remarked, "It is very hard to control the universe when you're insane." I responded, "Why not stop?" With determined resignation, he insisted, "Someone has to do it." The following day, he announced, with total conviction, "I am the high commissioner of cheese. Nobody in the world can eat cheese until I cut the first chunk at 6:45 a.m." Now what? This was new.

I called Elizabeth with the news, and she immediately took him off clonazepam, the tranquilizer he had been taking. Liver cancer had claimed so much of his liver that it no longer filtered his blood or detoxified chemicals. Controlling the world's cheese stopped after she took him off the drug. He still worked at controlling the universe. He gave me a grade of 185 percent for taking care of him, and I had another story to tell our friends.

I had always been David's projection screen, but now, I was also his spiritual companion As we staggered through months of facing death, *Infinity* was critical to both of us. The process of writing that book taught me monk language and monk think. When David was dying, I could understand him, and we had a book of directions for a monk's death. I listened, but he knew I could also translate. He could talk about the burning bush, the gentle whisper, about pseudo-Dionysius, and John of the Cross, and I would understand what he meant. I would understand his agony always beneath his rejoicing. I understood and quietly assured him, "You are still you." I looked at him and again thought, "How beautiful he is."

Nine days after we were given the new deadline, David finally became willing to talk about our life, and what it meant. The memories were so far from our current reality, and David was so weak, so tired, he seemed to be in a haze. But, as we talked about our best times, the really great events, important events, he perked up. We both remembered the day we met, January 19, 1967. David added some details about the restaurant and wondered how I got home. The Lyric Opera's production of *Lucia di Lammermoor* with Joan Sutherland and Luciano Pavarotti was another great event, and even bigger, the arrival of my Steinway B concert grand to our mountain home. In the midst of all these memories, some very long pauses. We laughed at each other and at us, much self-deprecating humor, much dark humor, and lots of silence. Then, we remembered the picnics at Ravinia's summer concerts and our sheer delight in building a new house from scratch.

Yet death never left us. In between the memories, David worried, "What happens if I faded out right now? What happens if I die right now?" He specified that when he died, he wanted me to personally call his friend Gene. Then life broke through again: we talked about our sing-alongs, which we thought were the very best of our memories. David said with emphasis, "Taking care of you was big." He had loved taking care of me, protecting me. Then he asked me if I would cut his hair. We were comfortably accepting each other, knowing each other, in this ordinary and affectionate conversation.

Then, abruptly changing the topic, he said, "You've done so well that I feel I can go." I told him, crying all the time, "I want you to be free. I will miss you, but I want you to be free." He thought it would be good to die after Christmas, stroking along with the Christmas liturgy without any ordinary ferial days. Then we talked about the earrings I would wear for the funeral. All sorts of trivial human stuff. With his typical long-range view, he concluded, "The big event is the totality of forty-eight years." David was breathing deeply—our conversations never ended, but I stopped and said we could continue later.

David's brain was still working, but on a different track. As he sat in his chair each day, restless, afraid he wouldn't be ready for God, I listened to him; he had strange thoughts, differing thoughts on sequential days. Since he was a young Carthusian, the Trinity had fascinated him. He remembered our island days in North Carolina and thought of the Trinity as the Cape Fear River crashing into the Atlantic Ocean. He began to think in colors; he saw eternity as blue. David thought one final phase had started. The next day he reflected, "Today is our last January 29, perhaps our last January day." I felt that this day, January 29, encapsulated the essence of David, philosopher, and God seeker.

On the next morning, David was thinking about this book, our dying book, and wanted to tell me what he thought about when he was alone, on condition that I would write the book. I said I probably would and recorded the conversation. He started by saying, "What I have learned thus far." He then explained that he is not able to use words when thinking about death, cannot put a coherent sentence together, cannot find a way to talk about death. Instead of words, he thinks in sounds, colors, silences. He sees a red ball; it is very vivid and represents death at the end of life. A black drape threatens to overshadow the red ball. Sometimes a beige color appears. He thinks about what he wants to do now, at the end of his life, but believes that things resolve themselves at the end.

The conversation has long pauses, his hands continually shake; when I say it could be the drugs, he emphasizes that it is anxiety. He doesn't know when he is going to die and is troubled because he doesn't understand how the queuing process works. I say nothing; I listen, totally focused on staying with him. He comments, "You are doing a terrific job." After a pause, he comments, "I don't see how it gets any bigger." I agreed, how could we possibly survive this incredibly prolonged, messy, and irresistible death.

David finds it harder and harder to manage his powerful, and unfamiliar, emotions. He is trying to bring it all together, to bring his life together, still trying to control his world, still a CEO. He continues to theorize, "God will be something never imagined, not anything we can imagine." Since he was twenty-three, he has been searching for God: not the Catholic God or any other religion's God, but his own God. He explains, "I built my God from spare parts." His God started as the God of an Irish Catholic monk, but he continued to search for Him in various religions. With laughter in his voice, he comments, "I wish I could think of something to make God smile." I told him that I was confident his infectious smile would make God laugh in delight.

Although he was paying attention to God, the intensity of our relationship never lagged. Later that day, January 30, he became anxious about my being present when he dies. After arguing about which aides should let me know when he is dead, he insists that he will die and I won't know. I keep telling him that the nurse will call me right after she calls hospice, but I can't get him out of this loop. My voice is getting desperate. Then we are quiet for a while. He keeps trying to get a plan in place for when he dies, but he is getting mentally exhausted trying to solve an unsolvable problem, to create certitude where there is none. He is failing to control when he is going to die. We keep going through this over and over again. I tell him I will ask the aides to call me after he gets ready for bed. He objects strenuously and angrily, "I'm in charge of me, as long as I'm alive, I want to be in charge of me." I am exhausted just listening to the recording years after his death, wondering how we both survived.

In the midst of this, he is looking good, apologizing for the bad smell in his room (from passing gas), joking ironically and laughing, dealing with aides, and watching golf on TV. He mentions how comfortable he is, but I am not comfortable. Stressed and worn out, I comment on the recording, "I'm so tired that I'm tripping and falling all over;" my voice is tight and steely.

We have passed our coping ability. We are no longer a team, and I am too depleted to orchestrate this messy dying process. He comments, "The coincidence of your exhaustion and my anxiety will coincide." I'm struck by our immense loneliness. We are both struggling. He asks who will walk me back to the apartment. He is happy when I call someone to walk me back.

On February 9, eighteen days before the deadline, we were back to our usual flirty sparring. He was still thinking about me, as well as God. He asked for my iPhone, wanting to record something: "This morning, after ruminating about my life, for the first time, I felt that our marriage was the most influential thing in my life, more than time in the monastery. So, congratulations, Nancy, for beating everything out, including the monastery. Are you happy about beating the monastery after almost fifty years of fighting it?"

Yes, I was happy to have beaten the monastery. It was a hell of a job for forty-eight years, but I won. A Pyrrhic victory. And I doubted that this was the final word on the matter.

A few days later, on February 13, he spent the entire day working at dying, determined to control his time of death. He told me not to call him or bother him. Waiting for him to call, I dozed off and dreamed David was bending over me, kissing me. I feared he was visiting me from the other side, and grieved. After waiting for twenty-three months, I wanted to be there at the end. When he called, he told me that he realized that it didn't make any sense to think about God. He concluded, "Don't try to understand anything, you just wait." Then, he concluded, "It is a challenge to belief and sanity to just wait." Summarizing his day, he commented, "We have all the pieces of the puzzle, end of the program. Not much time left in this life."

Then, another surprise. A week later, on February 22, the emotional spectrum changed, went radiant, for both of us. I walked into David's room, and his face lit up like the sun. The whole room seemed filled with all the joy and beauty and love in the entire world. We both simply looked at each other, feeling we had everything we wanted in that room. He again asked how long I wanted him to live, and I again told him I wanted him to live as long as we could communicate in any way. I wanted to feel the grip of his hand as he went to another place. After his death, David's room, saturated with love and anguish, lured me; every time I got near it, I was swept into desire. Until it was again occupied, I would visit the room. Sometimes an aide would stay with me as I sat on his bed, looked out the window and grieved.

Later, I wrote to my internet support group: "We continue half-day by half-day in *The Cloud of Unknowing*. Our relationship has become so intense that even three hours of wordless communication exhausts both of us." We no longer had conversations. We talked more and more in intense silence. Sometimes David talked, more or less coherently, and I listened. We rarely had a normal verbal conversation; in another three months, neither one of us talked. We did not need to talk; we had said everything, felt everything, and did not need words. We just needed to be in each other's presence. I needed his presence to be alive, to be myself. Not doing, not talking, just being. One of the five young men wrote to me, "By the gift of your witness, I am moved, impressed and above all helped and humbled." David pointed out that no one was more interesting to him than me, and of course, no one was more interesting to me than David.

The day of the six-week deadline, February 27, David called me sounding agitated and desperate; he had written something down, but he wanted to tell me himself. He had struggled with our relationship for forty-eight years and wanted to end the struggle. So, with angst, he said on the phone, "I love you with all my heart and soul. It is so hard for me to say that, but it is true." He was trying to give me what I needed, to resolve our competing needs. He anticipated that he would be torn apart when he died, saying, "God will be pulling on me, and I will be hanging on to you." In his letter to me that day, he said, "You have loved me freely, without merit, without reciprocity. With you with me, my death may be our couple's strongest and most lasting hours. I cannot do this—whatever it is—alone." As far as he could, David had resolved his conundrum.

Watching his mind deteriorate was the worst; logic and perspicacity were frequently gone. I made the decisions and struggled to maintain my emotional balance. Later that day,

David called me at 5:00 p.m., very anxious for fear he would die in his sleep without my holding his hand. He said he had lots to tell me but couldn't right then because the Super Bowl was about to start. I called the charge nurse to check on him, but he would not let her in his room. When I walked back to his room, he explained that his girth was expanding on both sides and to remember that. Then he asked me to "tell everyone that in the end, all will be clear." He added, "It is difficult to leave, death is taking a long time." He couldn't think about anything but his death, had not been able to since February 28, 2014, when we decided to seek no further treatment.

I wonder how I possibly survived as the wife of a dying monk who needed to be in control, but was no longer able to be in control. I was constantly confronting irrationality and dependency, while always trying to make sure David thought he was in control. I found it hard to separate the David I'd known from the angry, confused, and no longer on top of his judgment David. The two Davids switched back and forth, the signals to his brain erratic, no longer reliable. The switches occurred quickly, and, from my observation, not predictably: a liver that no longer filtered toxins, a kidney very possibly not functioning, a brain possibly cancerous. His visible body changing, feet more and more swollen, girth larger and larger, and face gradually changing from pure Irish to a puffy pear shape. At the time, I only saw my David. Now, when I look at the pictures I took, the physical deterioration of his body is brutally clear.

On Monday, exactly a year after our decision, I asked him if he wanted me to call Elizabeth for some antianxiety drugs. He said, "Thank you." After I called Elizabeth, the order for Haldol was sent—all was set. But when the floor nurse came in to discuss it with him, he raged that he had ordered both the hospice nurse and the floor nurse to be there for the discussion. He was infuriated about the terrible side effects that could result from Haldol and was confused about its purpose. I told him Elizabeth wanted to see if it would work; he responded, "Let her find another guinea pig," and then asked, "Who's Elizabeth?" When I tried to persuade him to talk to the floor nurse, he ordered me out of his room. I was grateful.

We had nearly three months to go.

11

THE LONG WAIT

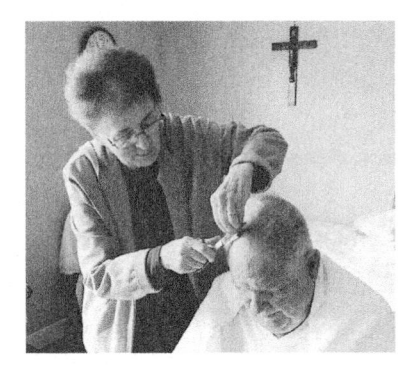

WE HAD MISSED the February 27 deadline, and gradually we resumed our normal weird way of living. I kept going to physical therapy, struggling with the bills and mail, and walking every day. David resumed his monk business. By mid-March, we forgot all about the two-to-six-week prognosis. The palliative care people did not even presume to make another prognosis. If they had, we would have ignored it. No one could understand why David was still alive; he was months past the projected death date. Nearly five years later, I realized why he was alive. He could not die until he had told me everything and put everything in writing.

With no other deadline in sight, we began the long wait, without a clue how long it would be. David moved on. "I'm finished with you," he said, "now I need to work on God." By the end of March, he totally focused on meditating on the face of God, his main agenda. But, when he tried to see the face of God, he only saw God's red shoes. This meditation continued over the week, but David just kept seeing God's red shoes, Ferragamo shoes. We laughed, another good story to share. While he was meditating, I tried to clear out his desk and files, asking him what I should keep; he reluctantly told me to throw out a list of clients that he still hoped to help. In the midst of all this paperwork, including a metal box of cashed checks from 1965, I showed him some current financial paperwork. He replied with disgust, "I'm getting ready to meet my maker and you show me brokerage records from Bernstein?"

During the long Milwaukee winter, he sat in his executive chair, looking out the window. Below his window was a parking lot with a dumpster at one end, but he saw neither. He watched the people walking their dogs on the street next to the parking lot. Most of all, he watched the children on the hill beyond the skeletal winter trees, sliding down the hill on their sleds, struggling and combating the snow. He liked watching one young boy who left his house, battled the snow, and finally slid down the hill. David thought that young man would always feel like a conqueror. More and more, he used images. At times, I thought he was becoming a poet. He had begun to talk in images.

Although he tried to focus exclusively on God, we had seemingly endless time to talk, about anything and everything. Now we could just reminisce and analyze. I wondered who I would become without David. In mid-March, I asked him who he would want me to be if he came back in ten years. David very cogently recorded a five-minute analysis—as he would have recorded a professional interview. He kept saying, "Don't change," and ended with the comment, "You have the weirdest deck of cards I've ever seen." Since he had interviewed thousands of people, quite an assessment.

I couldn't let him stop there. For another twenty-eight minutes, he explained his assessment: "No one else parallels you, your diversity of skills, your disparity of talents." He pointed out that this gift and curse meant no one could pigeonhole me, commenting, "They can't deal with it." He wondered what game I could play with this weird deck. What commitments should I make? I comment, "I don't join things, I start things, and I finish them. I create my own game." He wants me to talk about my own spiritual life, but suggests that I won't, that I will probably deny it. He infuriatingly reiterates: "It would be a terrible loss if you change your commitment to excellence." He recognizes that it will be painful, but still insists, "Don't change." He advises, "Do something that can't be done—then you have a chance of getting it right."

David's comments deeply validated me. He knew things that I didn't tell him. I had not realized how alert he was to my private life. I should have realized that he had very keen insight. When I forget who I am, I listen to this recording. I wonder if writing this book meets David's criteria of what can't be done; I certainly doubted that it could be done, and that I would be able to write it.

He said he was finished with me, but he kept thinking about me. On March 23, he called me to say, "Remember this. Every night before I go to sleep, I think of you, so if I die during the night, you will be here." Three days later, he called to say he was only waiting for me—for me to be ready for the funeral. He repeated this later: "I'm staying alive to make you safe at this retirement home or elsewhere." He had finally made the connection between loving God and loving me: "When I see the face of my maker, I will see you." He believed that I would be safe until he made room for me, joining him in another place. He wrote, "I will be with you constantly." Finally, David had resolved his conundrum. And I was finally in a more peaceful place. I had wanted David Maguire for forty-eight years, and now, in a sense, I had him.

In late March, a few weeks before David was able to communicate with the world outside his cell, he started having deliriums. Deliriums are characterized by extreme restlessness, illusions, and incoherence in thought and speech. They come suddenly and are reversible, usually caused by extreme illness or drug toxicity. No one had told me about deliriums or warned me about what to expect; they came as a surprise. All the Davids I'd known came and went: some of the deliriums were typical, some seemed peculiar to David. I wrote to Mary, "Life becomes stranger and stranger."

One day, after I had been with David for perhaps ten minutes, he told me, "I looked out the window this morning, and I saw Reinold, Ronnie, and Tom gutting an animal outside my window. I'd never seen anything like that before, and it frightened me." David had never met my dad, Reinold, and had never before mentioned him; Ronnie and Tom were my brothers who were both deer hunters. When he told me about the gutting, he still believed it had really happened. He decided: "This afternoon, you and I are going to every security store in Milwaukee to find the very best people to guard my room." I didn't know what to do, so I made an excuse to leave and called hospice. The receptionist asked, "Who are you?" I answered, "I'm David Maguire's wife." She said, "I can't talk to you if you're not a nurse." I was dumbfounded. The very next morning, I called our hospice and said, "There is no negotiation possible. I want you to change my name anywhere you have it in your documents to: Dr. Nancy Klein Maguire." They did. And that change helped me get help at the end.

David changed quickly and continually, from week to week, even day-to-day. I found it harder and harder to listen to him, to continually observe the degeneration of his mind. At times, I was completely frustrated at my inability to communicate—David no longer had words. I could not figure out what he wanted to hear and never knew what he understood. I tried sitting across from him in a chair—eyeball to eyeball. What had I wanted him to understand? I felt irritated, feeling shortchanged. Why hadn't he talked to me decades earlier? Why doesn't he ever ask about me? He was, of course, totally incapable of asking about me. Not his fault. These twenty-six months seem to have destroyed me, made me less than I wanted to be.

On April 5, Easter Sunday, always David's favorite day, the most mystical day, he analyzed my anger: "My dearest Nancy, feels good to write that. We were just huffing and tussling at the air and at each other. I knew all the huffing didn't mean a thing, just trying to keep our equilibrium by letting off steam. I love you. Nothing changes. I hope you are sure of that as I am." We still had another six weeks.

In mid-April, the president of the retirement home fired Lisa without warning, giving her one hour to leave the premises. Lisa, my main resource, had given me all her telephone numbers; in an emergency I could call her. She was not replaced. The president, a CFO (chief financial officer), took her place. On the same day, Lisa's future daughter-in-law quit her job as my helper in the apartment. I had to go to the president of the retirement home to get a replacement. We had no helper.

Then, another huge shift. Suddenly, David announced that he and his friend Ron had been planning a party; he was "having a blast." I don't remember David ever using a word like "blast" before. He had been trying to do all the things he had never done, and perhaps throwing a party was one of them. He definitely was having fun planning a party featuring Greek food, saganaki, perhaps like a high school celebration. Very few people in the retirement home knew what saganaki was, and that perhaps was part of the fun. David wanted to see all the people that he hadn't seen since he moved to assisted living.

David had a great time planning the party, deciding whom to invite, and what food to serve. He wanted to invite forty people. I protested. Sixteen months earlier, having cider and doughnuts with three people had exhausted him. I argued and argued and argued. On her April visit, while looking at me critically, Elizabeth said, "I think it is terrific that a dying man knows how to have fun." Plans for the party continued. I was recruited to give a speech at the beginning of the party. David wanted people to hear my voice.

I had become more and more voiceless during the twenty-six months. I was grieving, publicly, something sociably unacceptable. No one listened to me. The morning of the party, April 14, David called and said he wasn't sure he could make it. He didn't give a reason, but I suspected he wasn't ready for people to see him in his debilitated condition, and he suddenly realized that he was very tired. I called Ron who said we would go ahead and asked that I give my speech first. When I went to see David before the party, he said he wouldn't leave his room and would not see anyone. I stationed a friend/guard by his door to keep people from entering his room. Looking at pictures of the event, I estimate that twenty residents attended. Everyone who had come wanted to talk to David, at least to see him. I dreaded hosting this party. Miserable, awkward, I felt like an alien among these people I never could figure out.

The party was a fiasco. Ron took over, and I finally gave my speech in the midst of heavy wine drinking. I introduced myself as the silent partner of team Maguire, and again explained why I was committed to creating a culture of compassion. I concluded with the hope that the retirement home would become a compassionate community in my lifetime. No one listened enough to hear me, and I forgot to record it for David.

When I went back to David's room, he said, "I even failed to attend my own party." David had never failed at anything. I had tried and failed to keep him from this experience. That was the end of David's attempts to communicate with the world outside his own cell. After David had been weakened by cancer and exhausted himself, he and I had uninterrupted quiet time together. Mary wrote, "Stay strong. Focus on you. I think the end is drawing near."

The roller coaster ride became more turbulent, erratic, more heartbreaking. David now had been dying for twenty-five months. Following a surgery for liver cancer, David spent six days in the SICU, thirty days in the hospital, and another thirty-seven days in the medical center. He had been on intravenous meropenem for nine weeks. The second surgery and opioids exhausted his already damaged resilience. He had gone through a cocktail of drugs: Ritalin, clonazepam, Lyrica, tramadol, warfarin, a diuretic, and who knows what else. Since January 30, he had not been able to tolerate any kind of tranquilizer.

He had now exceeded his expected prognosis of eighteen months by seven months.

12

A MONK'S DEATH

DAVID'S medical power of attorney reverted to me on April 24, 2015. On that day, David entered his last entry in his day planner. The time between then and his death on May 18 was by far the most difficult, for both of us. David's speech was limited, he could not use the phone, could not write, we could do nothing but wait—he had earlier realized, "It is insane to just wait." When Continental Bank collapsed, and he had to terminate five thousand people, he was unhappy, but not unhappy like this. Until now, he had been able to move around in his cell, go to the bathroom alone, and move from his recliner to his bed. For the first time, on April 25, he had to use a walker to get out of bed. Later in the day, to his immense chagrin and anger, he defecated in bed, and the nurse had to change the sheets. He hated it. He was so ready to die.

David never lay in bed during the day; he sat in what he called his office chair, moving back and forth to his recliner. Three days later, April 27, he struggled to get from his recliner to the cot he had put in the room for me so I could spend the night. Once there, using both his hands, he tightly clasped mine. He smiled and looked happy. He was happy when I was with him. He often said to me, "I wish you could be with me more." His face lit up like sunshine when he saw me. Every day before I left, he said, "I love you, Toots." He was getting ready to leave me. I asked him, "When will we say goodbye?" He answered, "I will never say goodbye to you." When he was ready for bed the following day, he held my hands, looked at me through half-closed eyes, and I saw his entire soul, unguarded, uncontrolled. That soul was what I had loved. Then he closed his eyes and said, "I love you."

I called Gene to share this scene. I said, "this could be a paragraph in a book." Gene said, "it has to be a paragraph in a book. Many people have this experience, but they can't write about it. You can speak for them." David's job was to die, my job was to write the book.

We could only wait, locked in the sacred energy of death. He sat slumped over in his chair, waiting, day after day, after day, after day. We were in a place where time and speech stopped and nothing ever happened, nothing changed. We lived in a constant "now," the monk's *nunc*. His scraggly hair bothered him, he asked me to cut it. I called the nurse to get a pair of scissors and cut it while he grimaced, not wanting to hold still. The following day, he wanted me to get into bed with him. After I got into the cot, he put his left arm under me and held both my hands with his right hand. By this time, his face was so bloated that it had shape of a pear. His lips curled down, and he looked resigned. I was happy to be in bed with him again.

He continued to decline, becoming progressively weaker and less lucid. He would say to me, "I'm living so long because I want to give you more information before the funeral," or "I'm waiting for you to be ready for the funeral." By May 2, David was very happy to just lie on the bed and let me hold his hand. Before I left that day, he said we had to talk, he needed to talk about something very important, he needed my help. He asked the aide to leave, used his walker to move to his recliner, and started to tell me about four squares of different colors. He had identified the first three, but he needed my help with the fourth. He thought that if he identified the fourth color, he would be finished and could die. I had no field of reference for this and left, saying that we would work on the fourth color tomorrow. I was distraught watching his fine mind deconstructing.

As I write this, I'm back in #3307, seeing the single window looking out on the parking lot and dumpster, the incoherence of David's monk cell, the dingy blue-gray carpeting. I smell the typical hospital smell and remember the sweetness of David's body. His body was always warm. Remembering this, I again have to stop writing because my voice-activated software does not hear me when I cry. I feel nauseous, and I'm keeping the door to my office bathroom open.

The following day, his mind had shifted again. He was in another place, one I had not yet experienced. When I called him at 9:30 a.m., he replied with urgency, "I've been waiting and waiting for your call. I don't know what is going on. Everything is mixed up. I fired the aide. Come." He urgently explained, "I figured out what is wrong with time, the clock has twelve hours but there are really only ten hours." I alternated between talking to him on the telephone and trying to get an aide. Finally, he said, "Come soon." I pulled on a sweatshirt and cords and went to the assisted living facility — without bath or breakfast. It took me a nine-minute walk to get there. When I got to his room, he was sitting smugly in his business chair wearing his oxygen mask. He had had trouble breathing. He said, "I got everything done before you got here." He had had a panic attack.

I said I needed to get a shower, and he said, "There is a shower right here." I was very tired, unclean, and still waiting for the staff to find an aide. David had already fired the first one, then a second and third. At about 1:00 p.m., David decided to fire everyone—a blanket firing. When I reminded him that he liked the aide Barbara, he said, "Fire one, fire all—that is only fair." I said, "David, you can't do that." With total authority, he announced, "This is my premises, and I have my power of attorney. I want everyone out of here. I don't need anyone." Then he started to make a list of things he wanted the aides to do for him. He broke the agreed-upon rule and went to the bathroom without asking an aide to help him. I told him, "You fire all, you fire me." I left.

I went back to the apartment and my friend Iris persuaded me to attend an anniversary celebration in the building. To my amazement, Nancy Klein Maguire was still alive, buried under the debris of David's long death. Everyone was excited to see me dressed up and working the room, delighted that I had come back. They probably knew it was temporary; I certainly did. When I returned to the apartment, I was unsteady and frightened.

The next morning, my telephone rang three times. Each time I answered it, David said, "This is a wrong number." He called again and asked me to come to his room. When I went inside the room, he knelt down, very awkwardly and dangerously, and kissed my feet. He said, "That's how it's done, isn't it?" He explained that he had planned to practice, but he was afraid he would fall down and not be able to get up. He told me that he didn't know how else to tell me how sorry he was for kicking me out of his room. He hoped, "it is the disease." He did not unfire all the staff he'd fired the day before, but I assured him, "You're still you." I was both amused and horrified by the changes in my formerly uptight, proper, and reserved husband.

The next day, David had a premonition that he was going to die that night. After the aide got him into bed at 5:30, he turned on his side, took my hand, and with his lids half open, he looked at me with totally unguarded eyes—nothing held back, no guardedness, no attempt to control, no facade. He knew he might die that night, and he was saying, "This is all I am, and I am yours." Then he said, "I love you," before going to sleep. And I stumbled out of the room with tears blocking my sight. It seemed sacrilegious to look into another person's soul. It was like seeing the face of God.

David and I were past medicine, past theology, and even emotion. We lived in a different place, in a different kind of time. After walking hand in hand with David toward our death, I knew him as few human beings know each other. I could finally accept his human incompleteness, his emotional voids, and his death.

Soon after, I took a long, cold walk down Prospect Avenue. I realized how alone I was and went back to David's room to be part of a human connection, however short-lived. He asked me for a few things, and let me borrow some of his clothes, mine were wet with sweat. The depth of my loneliness began to sink in. My nights were filled with horror at the thought of a world without David, being utterly alone in an indifferent universe. I would no longer be the center of anyone's universe; I was always number one with David, and there was no number two, three, or four. No one looking out for me, no one caring about my health or well-being. During the twenty-six months, I had lost emotional contact and every-day connections with my prior life. I was no longer aware of any life prior to David's liver cancer diagnosis.

On his way back from a conference in Phoenix, Ressa stopped again and went with me on my last daily check. We found David with John, a resident who was a friend of David's. He was explaining to John, with great conviction and detail, that the authorities kept changing his room. With glee, he told John that the staff moved all his things to a different room, trying to make him think it was the same room. But he had figured it out. John left, and I told Ressa to get some dinner while I stayed with David.

The aide scheduled to be with David during the last shift of the day had not shown up. David was in a deep delirium, and Ressa and I stayed with him until around nine. Then, in spite of his confusing delirium, David told Ressa to walk me home. I fell asleep very quickly, and Ressa returned to David's room and stayed the entire night. The staff had agreed to check on David every half-hour. Ressa verified that, again, no one had checked on David during the night.

With Lisa gone, I had no one to call. The president had replaced Lisa with a team of nurses who alternated being on call. No one knew the identity of the nurse on call or their contact numbers. I called my lawyer, asking her to obtain an emergency cell phone number for the charge nurse. Later that day, I asked a staff member for help in finding 24/7 nurses, which David needed when he was in delirium. The president herself responded with a telephone call, saying, "David will never have 24/7 nurses. I saw him last night, I'm seeing him again next Tuesday." She then told me that they were having a meeting about me about my overanxiety and overconcern about David. I quietly told her, "Yes, the palliative care NP, the hospice nurse, the floor nurse, and myself are having a meeting. You are not invited."

Ten minutes later, Todd, the hospice assessor, reported that

David needed 24/7 care and also expected that quite soon, David's medical power of attorney should transfer to me. A few hours later, Elizabeth came to see David. She reported to my lawyer: "He is in a delirium, and he is dying like someone in a hotel room, with neighbors occasionally stopping by." I did not get a cell phone number for the charge nurse. A year later, the medical center became so poorly staffed that the residents formed a secret committee to try to get proper staffing.

In an almost illegible letter to me, David commented, "Dealing with the president shows a lot of grit and courage. You gave her the real story with your memos and did not give tit for tat." He added, "And you kept me in my place. You listened. Told me that you were not going to take my advice and had no trouble. I slept well last night. The real you is back." David was very aware of the lack of staffing in the medical center, and of the difficulties I had with the staff.

The next day, David was unusually lucid. When I told him on the phone that I was not alone, he knew that meant that our lawyer was with me. When I got to his room, he told me, "I don't care if you overcome or undergo my death." He then said very factually, seriously, "This is the end of my life." He still tried to write one last letter to people important to him. He reflected how odd it was to send a letter from a dead man. He later asked me, "Why hasn't there been a funeral?"

About this time, he had a delirium that many dying people have. When I went to see him in late afternoon, he was telling an aide to pack all his things. He explained to me, "I know they are going to move me again, and I have to get everything safely out of here." He told me to get his wallet and car keys. I assured him I already had taken them. David replied, "And you have to get a gun." I told the aide to take David's clothes to our apartment; there were very few of them, and they were well worn. He relaxed when he realized that all his things were safe. Those were hard days. We wanted it to be over, but all we could do was wait. It seemed that death would never come. His ambiguity about God and his wife continued; he said, "God will be reaching for me, and I will be hanging on to Nancy."

On May 11, a week before he died, he tossed everyone but me out of his room, lurched over to the cot from his recliner, and wanted me to stroke his back. He struggled with the bedclothes, positioning and rearranging my hand so that it was flat. He was silent for a long time, breathing slowly and heavily. I thought he might be sleeping, or perhaps dying. But then he woke up restlessly agitated and said, "I have so much work to do. I've so much work to do." Eric, the hospice social worker, had told me David would not die until we both wanted it. Very ill and exhausted, he could not stop working. I said to David, "You have done everything, everything, perfectly. There is nothing left for you to do. Your only job is to die." His entire body relaxed, his face collapsed, and he fell asleep. He was determined to die, but he kept trying to communicate. Very close to the end, he left a confused voice message telling people how to get in touch with him.

The following day, I asked John's wife Bobby to walk with me for my evening check, and on the way, the aide called me and said David wanted me, and that he could not walk. We moved more quickly, and when I got there, the only word he could say was "pill," just once. I suspected this was the end of his life. I sent the aide for the charge nurse and called hospice: "This is Dr. Nancy Klein Maguire. My husband is a patient of Suzanne Smith, and I want a nurse here stat." She asked, "What is the problem?" I said that if I knew that, I wouldn't be calling. Todd, the assessor, called back immediately. The charge nurse had just arrived, and we both talked to Todd on my iPhone. We agreed that I should give David morphine, his first dose. Todd arrived quickly. Bobby stayed in the parlor to give me privacy.

After shutting off all the lights but the bathroom light, I shut the door to the room and quietly held his hand. The morphine had knocked him out, and he was resting quietly, nearly asleep. I didn't let Todd in until he agreed not to wake David and to examine him in the dark. He did so very skillfully and compassionately. He was concerned about me and asked me how I was. I calmly and factually told him, "I have seen him die before." I was ready. I joined Todd in the nurse's office, and he told me David probably had one to two days to live.

Bobby walked me back to our apartment. She wanted me to take a shower, but first I needed to make some phone calls. I called Gene, and finally Ressa. I told Ressa to get on the next plane; he objected, "I have four projects due tomorrow." I responded, "Get here as soon as you can." Then, I laid out my clothes for the next day and finally took a shower and went to bed.

At 7 a.m. the next morning, I found David sitting comfortably in his recliner wearing his oxygen mask. Ressa arrived at noon. After being gone for six days, he found the changes in David startling. David didn't realize that he had just lost the use of his legs, he had been walking in his room, sometimes with a walker. He kept trying to get out of bed, trying to walk. I pressed my core muscles against the edge of the bed, keeping him in bed. The look on his face said he was devastated by this final blow to his independence. After we moved him to his recliner, he stayed there. By late afternoon, when he wanted to move to the cot, he told the aide exactly how he should be moved, step-by-step, he was good at spatial directions. She stood in front of him, crossed her arms, and said, "Mr. Maguire, this is how we do it." She grabbed his feet and Ressa took him under the arms. But David's weight was in his midriff, heavy with cancer, so after a brief moment, they had to quickly lower him to the floor.

I kept reassuring David, "This is not your fault. You told them what to do." None of us knew what to do with his very heavy body, so I went to the second floor to find a charge nurse.

I announced, "We dropped someone on the third floor." I didn't give my name or that of the dropped patient, but she immediately got up and followed me. As we neared David's room, she said, "Not Maguire!" She really meant, "not again." David had not been an easy patient in this assisted living place.

When she and I got to the room, everyone laughed, including David. We found the situation absurd, and it felt good to let go of some of the tension. She called for a hoyer lift, and with much struggling, the entire group, by this time six or seven people, got the leather sling under David. I held his hand and kept repeating, "This is not your fault. They did it." He relaxed and, I think, rather enjoyed the ride through the air to the cot. He again said with great energy, "I hope I will die tomorrow." Ressa and I hoped he would too, so we could all remember this last time of laughter, and David being such a good sport.

The next morning I went to David quickly. He asked me to grab his hand and pull him out of bed. He had decided to put on his shoes and pants and tie. He said decisively, "Then, let's get out of here." He did not understand his situation. Dying people often have the illusion they can get dressed and leave. He had been eating well, pretty much ordering what he wanted, and now he wanted something to eat; he knew exactly what he wanted, but he couldn't find the name. I kept suggesting things that he usually could eat and liked to eat, but none of them were what he wanted. He was desperately trying to find the correct word, miserably confused why he couldn't find it. I just wished he would die quickly. We so wanted it to be over.

On Saturday afternoon, Ressa and I continued to spell each other. We were glad it was a weekend, no floor nurse or administrator to get in our way. My friend Iris walked me over from our apartment, and we talked for a while in the adjoining room. I asked David if Iris could wave at him. He nodded and even allowed her to kiss his forehead. He seemed relaxed and peaceful. But by late afternoon, David had again clenched his teeth shut and refused to take any medicine, as he had when I called hospice. The charge nurse gave me a vial of Haldol and told me to do what I could; as a nurse, she could not compel him to take medicine. She went to call hospice in exasperation, adamant that crisis care be brought in that night—she had other patients.

Within five minutes, a bright young nurse who'd been nearby came. After she examined David, she and I met with the charge nurse in her office. The hospice nurse wanted to take David to one of their own facilities, where he would have constant care. Since David had repeatedly insisted that he wanted to die in his cell, I told her that I had promised to never put him in an institution. Then I also refused let her give him drugs intravenously, another promise. I was thankful that our lawyer, who had the second POA, was available to validate my decision by phone.

While we were talking in the nurse's office, Ressa had found a parfait that David liked. He did the airplane trick that parents use to make children eat. David opened his mouth and ate. As soon as I returned, I sat very close to David with the vial of Haldol, and Ressa made a big loop with the parfait, and every time the spoon went by, I put a drop of Haldol in it. By the time the vial was empty, David was very happy and lying down.

After returning again to check on David, the hospice nurse explained that they did not have the staff to give David a round-the-clock nurse, but she arranged for a hospice nurse to come every four hours to give him two sticks each of Haldol and morphine. Both medications come in liquid and stick form.

I went home and slept. Ressa checked on David during the night and found he was restless and in pain. Morphine and Haldol every four hours had not been enough. He could not sleep and had several uncomfortable hoyer lifts during the night. Ressa woke me at 4:00 a.m., I insisted I needed sleep, but by 5:00 a.m., the two of us, working a landline and two cell phones, started calling hospice, the charge nurse, palliative care, and the medical oncologist.

I went to David's room with my cell phone. I was ready to do my job of getting David safely buried. To do this, I had to block off emotion: to insulate myself, for David's sake, and to preserve my emotional integrity. I found David in his recliner. The calls started being returned. The crisis care nurses arrived with great energy. I went into the hallway and told them, "You must remember three things: he has his own medical power of attorney, it is his room, and he had been a monk. You must only whisper in his room." I showed them a picture of a monk from the monk book. The chief critical care nurse got it. She gave me two sticks, one of Haldol and one of morphine, to give David, saying, "I will come in the room in fifteen minutes." I gave her my phone to take the incoming calls. She went to check with the charge nurse on the availability of drugs.

I think it was about 8:00 a.m. when she was ready to see David. When I allowed her in his room, he was still sitting in his recliner. She was very tall, so she knelt down next to the recliner so that her head was on the same level as David's. He had not seen this nurse before, but he reached out his hand, grasped hers, and graciously said, "I'm so glad to see you." She left, and after a while, another hospice nurse appeared; she had been informed of David's requirements. We established the routine that we kept up during that day. Since he would only open his mouth for me, I started giving him two sticks each of morphine and Haldol every hour, four in all. The hospice nurse brought me the four sticks, I put them under his tongue, and then she squirted water in his mouth. I explained to David that I had hired a special assistant because he complained that I always spilled water on him. After she had finished, I would say, "Now, get out of here." David believed that I alone was in control of his drugs. I suspect it is odd for a spouse to administer the drugs. But, I wanted the job, I had the responsibility, the right, to birth him into death.

We kept this up throughout the day, even though the hospice administrator called me, telling me Medicare would not pay for David's care because I had forced him to take drugs. I needed the laugh. Friends occasionally called to see if I needed anything. I probably called for some pills for myself. I kept this up until David was unconscious, ostensibly unaware of me. I don't remember any emotion, but I wanted to stay with David. I felt better when I was with David. At death, there is such thin air between worlds: for a short time, David was in both worlds, the other world lingered. I wanted to stay with David in both worlds, but, I was falling asleep on the cot. An aide had come to help turn David, and she insisted I get some sleep.

I don't remember how I got back to the apartment, and I don't remember what I did when I returned. Ressa probably walked me back. He had invited visitors to the apartment who were chatting about high school days: I said in a loud voice, "I don't want to hear any voices in this apartment." Ressa took them out, and I think they all went to dinner at the Pfister Hotel. I probably slept.

The next day, I dressed with care, knowing it would be my last day with David. My cell phone had not rung during the night, so I knew he was still alive. I don't remember who escorted me, but when I got there around 8:00 a.m., David seemed conscious and kept squeezing my hand. I told him again and again, "It is almost over, by tonight it will be over." I repeatedly said, "You did a good job, we did a good job; we did an even better job than we did with your mother." I assured him, "I will be all right. I will kick ass if anyone messes with me." The aide in the room laughed quietly. At about 10:00 a.m., I read the last page of the monk book, a quotation from St. John of the Cross important to David: "What will take place on the other side when all for me will be overturned into eternity;

I don't know. I believe, I believe only that a great love awaits me."

David was having increasing difficulty breathing, arching his back, lurching forward. The aide lifted his head so that I could put a pillow under it. When that didn't help, the nurse and the aide crawled under the bed, trying to adjust the hospital bed so that his head would be higher. They were having great difficulty, and I worried about their backs. So shortly after 10:28, I left to get help from the floor's nursing center. I announced, "I need muscle," and a very heavyset, muscular woman followed me. I had been gone just forty-four seconds. When I reentered David's room, the hospice nurse said, "He just passed, time of death 10:30 a.m." In the forty-four seconds that I was gone, he died; his spirit simply left his body. He had not said goodbye.

After sending a text to Gene and the monks, I shut everyone out of the room, and I sat next to the bed, holding his hand, saying repeatedly, "David, you should've waited for me, I was just gone for a minute. I didn't leave you. I did not abandon you." I was terrified that he thought I had abandoned him. I vaguely remember that people came and went in the room. Eric, the hospice social worker, was concerned about me and asked me if I would see the chaplain, who came in for a second or two. Then the two aides who had been with David came in and put their arms around my head and said, "We are here any time you want us." And they were. His body was still warm. He looked as if he might just be asleep. A dying David was hugely preferable to a dead David. He had been dying for so long I didn't think he would ever really die.

Then, when after over two hours, he had not breathed, I let the undertakers enter at 12:55 p.m. The undertaker was a familiar and supportive figure, and I was glad he was the one who entered the room. I watched as he and his brother carefully wrapped David in dark blue corduroy blankets and transferred him to a gurney. They left.

Then, I left.

When my monk husband finally died, I found it hard to believe that I was still breathing. I had been hit by the worst event of my life and I was still alive. We had both been dying during those twenty-six months. I had not expected to survive, did not know what parts had survived. Still don't.

13

REJOICE

Ressa and I collected David's things and with the help of Eric and the chaplain took them back to our apartment. Then, without pause, Ressa and I made sure that the death announcement on the bulletin board in the lobby was exactly the way David had wanted. He had been very precise about the photograph. We brought David's choice, a picture of him sitting in bitterly cold weather on our mountain patio, and insisted that the administration print a new death announcement.

Then, we ate a pizza. Later that day, Ressa and I walked the pier jutting into Lake Michigan. After walking fifteen minutes on the pier, I looked up and could barely see the retirement home in the distance. Momentarily, I felt real. I might have been at our mountain home or our family cottage in southern Wisconsin. I was safe, away from the retirement home. We probably ate more pizza for dinner, but early in the evening, I collapsed into bed, immediately falling into sleep.

As usual, I woke up at 2:00 a.m., thinking in anguish: "I can't do this. I can't keep doing this. I can't do this again. I cannot go through one more day." Then, words rushed through my mind like a lightning bolt: "David is dead." My body collapsed in relief, and I fell into a deep sleep. I broke the sleep the next day to finalize the obituary and funeral arrangements. Since Memorial Day was on May 25, I put the funeral off until May 26. More time, another day or so, to prepare for that ordeal.

In the funeral home, I was able to see David's dead body and face. Seeing his face seemed essential. I did not see how I could continue to live without seeing his face. He still looked like himself; he might yet be sleeping. I had planned to visit the funeral home and see his face every day until the funeral, but since the body was not embalmed, I was not able to see it again. Returning from the funeral home, I collapsed into a four-day sleep, getting up only to eat and other essentials. I didn't speak to anyone during those four days. On May 20, Dom Leo, one of the five young men, now old men, wrote, "It has been a long journey for you both. You have been very brave."

When I woke from my long sleep, I stayed in the apartment unless I was with Ressa. My brother Tom's wife was ill, and I insisted that he not come to the funeral. He promised to come afterwards, and he did. After a few days, I looked in the mirror and sent Ressa to get some hair color, a first-time job for him, maybe someone came to cut my hair, and a neighbor helped me choose what to wear for the funeral. Since it was warm, I could wear my lightweight outfit rather than the heavy monastic one. I was still so exhausted that my doctor authorized some uppers to get me through the funeral. I was distraught for fear I would cry in a judgmental environment, but Mary told me, "No matter what you do, people won't like it. Just get through it."

At the suggestion of the funeral director, Ressa and I drove to The Gesu an hour early and went straight to the bride's room, secluded from the approaching mourners. The room was very comfortable; I lay down on something like a flat sofa, and Ressa sat in an upholstered armchair. We both felt relaxed and were joking around a bit.

When the congregation was in place, I went down to the nave of the church, hugged all the waiting pallbearers, and braced myself for the long walk down the aisle. As I walked behind David's coffin, the organist was playing Bach's "Jesu, Joy of Man's Desiring" on the magnificent old organ. Tears were coming down my face, tears of grief, fear, confusion, but what I really felt was pride. Proud that David and I had done what even we doubted we could do. Also, oddly, I felt like a bride. We had stayed the course for twenty-six months, stayed together without faltering, without looking back, steady in our decision. I wasn't fully aware of who was there, and I'm still not, but, while tears streamed down my face, everyone was looking at me. I braced myself and walked to the front of the church. Gene and Mary were in the front pew, waiting for me.

Our Jesuit friend Nicky presided at the funeral, wearing the very colorful and primitive stole that David had asked him to wear for his funeral. The funeral went exactly as David had directed—except for the homily, which even David couldn't control, or have predicted. Everyone had a copy of David's Mass of Christian Burial, containing exactly what David had wanted, including the readings and responses. Holding the heavy hymnals in the pews, the Episcopalians from the retirement home and David's colleagues belted out the responses.

My brother Peter did the second reading from Philippians 3:8–15, which ends with David's favorite mantra: "Forgetting what lies behind and straining forward to what lies ahead, I press on toward the goal." Father Nicky then read the Gospel. David had chosen Mark:25-34 which insisted on the need to care for people. David had cared for people his entire life, whether professionally or informally. After the Gospel reading, everyone boisterously sang the joyous Celtic Alleluia.

Following the schedule for the Mass of Christian Burial, our Jesuit friend Nicky did the homily; normally he would have spoken of David. But, for this particular funeral, he improvised and simply said, "In honor of David, we will meditate."

The church was roaringly quiet. No one knew what to do. Everyone looked at their copy of the Mass of Christian Burial and didn't see any directions. Nothing was happening. Silence. What were we supposed to be doing? People were anxiously looking at their watches. Silence. A few started meditating. One minute, another half minute, two minutes, another three-quarters of a minute, another minute, three minutes. What to do? Another minute. Approaching the five-minute mark.

People who go to funerals always try to do the right thing, especially in church. A Jewish couple was breaking out in a sweat. Six minutes. By this time, some people were actually meditating. I kept cranking my head to see what was happening. I was delighted that David finally had what he wanted: silence. Nobody was interrupting him, even I was not interrupting him, no one was disturbing the silence. He certainly did not expect ten minutes of silence, but I think he would have been delighted. Six minutes, seven minutes, eight minutes, nine minutes, and finally, at ten minutes, our Jesuit friend Nicky got up and the service continued. A gasp of relief from the congregation.

After that, my Jewish friend Nici read the prayers of the faithful. She read beautifully, reading all the prayers straight through. I had not told her, because I didn't remember, that after each prayer of the faithful, a whole string of other prayers was supposed to be said. The Catholics in the congregation were confused and slightly upset, looking around to see what was happening. But our Jesuit friend Nicky went straight on with the service. Beatrice and Iris brought the gifts to the altar in preparation for Communion. It was so good to have my friends with me. A priest friend of David's helped give out Communion while everyone sang "On Eagle's Wings."

The eulogy, called a remembrance to satisfy the bishop, was written by Gene but read by another friend. After remembering all of David's considerable accomplishments, the eulogy concluded: "Several of you have told Dave they will always be there for Nancy, whenever and wherever." Gene had consulted with David's colleagues before making that statement. The eulogy ended, "This is a real commitment. Rest assured Dave—we will be there for her." David had told Gene how comforted he had been by this assurance. I was greatly enheartened by the funeral ceremony. I thought all those people celebrating David would be my friends in the coming months. I was a very naive widow. Except for Gene and Mary, the entourage of David's colleagues permanently disappeared soon after the funeral luncheon.

At this point, Father Nicky moved into the aisle next to David's coffin, took off the white pall covering it, blessed the coffin with holy water, and then incensed it with a thurible. As he did this, he sang what David and I had called the *In Paradisum*: "May the angels lead you into paradise. . . . The choirs of angels receive you as Lazarus, may you have eternal rest."

Finally, the pallbearers came to the front of the church and started moving the coffin to the nave. I followed the coffin. The organist was blasting out Beethoven's *Ode to Joy*. As I walked out, I could see the people in the congregation. Many said I looked totally different than I had when I entered the church. Reaching the nave of the church, I hugged more people. I was heartened by the rejoicing and mourning of all these friends of David. The entire funeral was so David Maguire that Father Nicky and I, and others, were confident that David was actually present. I didn't allow any photographs or recordings. I wanted it to be a *nunc* performance, experienced only by those present. And I suspect those who were present have not forgotten it.

Two days later, we took David's body and coffin to my hometown cemetery in Sun Prairie, Wisconsin. Our Jesuit friend Nicky drove to Sun Prairie to officiate at the interment, putting his arm around me when that huge cement block was put over the coffin. The $250 coffin was buried under our very expensive tombstone. David's body was put to rest under his half of the tombstone carved with just one word: "Rejoice."

So, I began my life as The Monk's Widow, alternately grieving and rejoicing, working earnestly to earn my half of the tombstone, engraved with just one word: "Truth."

EPILOGUE

Today is a brilliantly sunny day with fierce winds. I'm in my office at our mountain home, sitting at the desk where I wrote *An Infinity of Little Hours* and most of this book. I'm in the first months of covid, and death again dominates life. But life can't be stopped. I see it emerging all over. Daffodils I planted in 2007 are finally blooming; the trees I had been nurturing since 1996 are beginning to leaf out. Like everyone, I'm searching for supplies for the house, empty since Fall.

I returned to the Allegheny Mountains a few days after the

one-year anniversary of David's death. I came with my computer and notes, unrealistically expecting our home to be the same as when we left. After a five-year absence, I expected to go straight to my office and start this new book. When I got out of the car, I saw that the garage door had gone missing, and scraps of metal littered the entranceway. When I entered the house, I found it mice-ridden, filled with mold, and with a dangerous oil leak. Although we had paid $500 a month to a caretaker to protect our home, the property had been trashed.

Yet, in the morning, I could see my trees, appallingly in need of pruning, but alive. Five years of weeds had disappeared the flowerbeds. But, every time I opened a door or closet, evidence of life rushed out. David's desk was cluttered with golf tees and scorecards. His clubs were in their usual place, and my office in the same mess as when I left five years earlier. I was confused by the pink cancer pins scattered around. David's long death had blocked out my breast cancer. Hard to think that breast cancer had ever been important. My friend Iris called when she heard what had happened to my home. She asked, "does it still make you happy?" Yes. It did. I was home.

I remembered that we had not always lived in death; we had had a life. I couldn't stop David's death, but I was determined to save our home and immediately went to work putting it back together. I tried putting our moldy clothes in the sun, but when that did not work, I started putting all of them, both David's clothes and mine, into the largest black garbage bags available. I needed to get them out of the house quickly to cut the smell of mold; I sent nine bags to the local animal shelter for fumigation and resale. A realtor who knew the house told me I would get a nickel on a dollar if I tried to sell the property. He said fixing it was not worthwhile, but I found a local contractor who was horrified at the state of the house and immediately put in an emergency call to stop the oil leak. When the various subcontractors came, they recognized the caretaker by his work, or lack of work. The house was in such ill repair that the contractor did not want the work. I persuaded him, and put him in touch with some of our workmen.

I had to leave the house while the exterminators flooded it with lethal pesticides. Under the direction of Gene, I continued to supervise the work by telephone, while creating a paper trail with the pest control company. In the spring, I returned to the mountains via Amtrak and began clearing out closets, drawers, the garden shed. Two people from the contractor's team worked after their jobs to clean the house and to rescue the landscaping. The landscape architect told me, "I don't have time to do this, but I don't want you to think everybody in the county is like the person who destroyed your home." They were remarkable. All the new subcontractors knew the story, and I suspect that they were trying to make up for the bad caretaker. A year later, our home was again habitable. I cleared out our retirement home apartment, moved from Milwaukee, and put all our furnishings back in place. Everything was as it had been before we left for Milwaukee in 2011. Except David.

I'm writing this during the beginning of the pandemic. As everyone, I'm fearful. David worried about whether he was ready to meet his maker. I worry whether this book will be published before the world becomes oblivious to books. And, does it matter? Is my job already over? I continue to struggle with the mystery of God, the mystery of my life and death with David. I'm still trying to find my own way to God, without David. The pandemic makes this even more difficult, but sometimes, I find her/him or she/he finds me. I have been alone in my mountain home for nineteen months, living like a hermit. I've had plenty of time to think about my life, our life, reflecting on my life and death with David.

A few days ago, my brother and editor, Tom Klein, asked me,

"What did you get out of this?" It's a fair question. What I got out of this particular death is invaluable, but came with an overwhelming cost. Being a death partner is the most difficult of human tasks. If David had simply had a heart attack or stroke and died quickly, I would not have been so stressed, exhausted, so defeated. But neither would I have had all the deeply satisfying conversations, all the insights into who we had been and who we were becoming. What had we accomplished? What should I carry forward? Dying with David made me accept the act of dying. I am more prepared for my own death, knowing what to expect emotionally and mentally. I understand the sheer aloneness of dying, no matter who might be holding my hand. I can accept that I will probably be dying alone—even David may not be there.

I knew David as well as any wife knows her husband. Dying with him for twenty-six months created a different pitch of knowing, communication with no guardrails, wordless conversations, intuitive understanding. Years, decades, of arguing ended with respect, love, and acceptance. I think that's big—even if it took forty-eight years to get there. Although I am missing fifty percent of myself, the remaining fifty percent is learning to tolerate a continuous sense of loss. I never stop missing David, but I keep moving in different directions, sometimes taking his place. I'm becoming less angry at him. The more I tolerate the complexities of this particular grief, the more David seems to be present, to be a shadow presence, a companion of sorts. Birthing David into death was a long and difficult labor, but the birth was beautiful, and that is what I live on.

Our mountain home, the Maguire retreat house, continues to be my emotional and spiritual home. On warm summer evenings, working in my upstairs office, I hear a car coming up the road. I go to the bathroom window at the end of the hall and talk for a while to the UPS man below. With the window open, the mountain evening pours into my house. I go back down the hallway and return to my office. In the quiet mountain evening, I realize that I am as complete as I will ever be. I keep an apartment in Washington, D.C., near the Folger Shakespeare Library, my professional home since 1981, yet I keep coming back to our mountain home.

ACKNOWLEDGMENTS

Tom Klein provided editorial advice as early as the summer of 2018. When I was totally confused, I would send him a draft. He would text back, "I can't possibly fix this, there too many errors." But I kept at it, and eventually, when he would say, "classic," I would know I was on the right track. As a retired publisher, my brother has been very helpful in publication decisions.

After I bitterly complained that no one in the Folger Shakespeare Library was willing to read a book about the act of dying, Michael Witmore, the director, offered to read two chapters of *The Monk's Widow*. He read the first and last chapters with great excitement, asking for more. During the next four years, he would periodically get a draft of a chapter, as clean as I could make it. He asked for my second chapter, and he got it, and he insisted I write the preface. They are his. He has been a constant source of encouragement and advice.

David Ressa was not only physically present during David's death, he was present by phone and email as I started to write. He read terrible draft after terrible draft with patience and encouragement, as well as frequently doing searches for me and being generally available. He also proofread several times. More than all that, when I'm totally confused and out of hope, David is the person I call, and he is always there.

My friend and physical therapist Daniel Baumstark read my first draft. I was terrified to have anyone read it, but when he finished, he said, "wow." Validation. William P. Williams and

Nachman Davies read and commented on early drafts. Gene Croisant has been a constant source of encouragement and read many early chapters. Lee Elliott, also a writer, read chapters from the very beginning, as well as several complete drafts. Her husband Bill made the cover possible, taking a high-resolution photo of the oil painting. Jana Troutman-Miller was a continual enthusiast, reading various drafts and providing reliable suggestions and corrections. Dr. Joan Gibson, bioethicist, read early chapters and the first complete draft with keen insight and perspicacity.

During the worst of the writing process, Amanda Held Gorman and Emily Miller encouraged me to continue writing, even to write the death chapter. My brother Peter also encouraged me to keep writing. Gorman read several complete drafts with great care, finding a gross repetition, as well as pointing me to new sources. Beatrice Belda Pronley read several drafts and was always available when David was dying, and continually thereafter.

Anne Horwitz did a very careful editing of the book. Andrea Schmidt taught me about self-publishing. Tammy McDonald, besides creating my website, did all manner of IT jobs which were way beyond my skill. Will Cesarei my computer person since December 2016, has always been available wherever I am, no matter what disaster has happened. Amy Rogers Nazarov is teaching me everything I never knew about selling a book through social media.

Mary Karr's *The Art of Memoir* gave me courage during my initial PTSD struggles, predicting what to expect and diagnosing the trauma of other memoirists. I read *The Art of Memoir* every day, as some people read the Bible.

THE STORY OF THE COVER OF THE MONK'S WIDOW

On a July afternoon in 2003, I went to an art fair in Bath County, will Virginia. I returned several times to look at "The Long Walk" by an artist named Laura Loe. In her oil painting, a woman in a red coat trudges up a steep hill, moving towards the woods, alone. The slope looked just like my slopes, and the trees could have been my trees. I am an Ent and loved to wander around the woods. I couldn't resist the painting, but it cost more than I'd ever paid for an artwork. I couldn't make myself buy it.

Still thinking about the painting, I dragged my husband

THE STORY OF THE COVER OF THE MONK'S WIDOW

David to the art fair. He looked at "The Long Walk" and said, in amazement, "that's you." It was the last day of the fair, and the staff was carrying out the unsold paintings. David rushed over and insisted, "We want this painting." By evening, the painting was hanging in our bedroom. Ten years later, as David was dying, we had "The Long Walk" sent to us at his death place in Milwaukee, Wisconsin. After David died, I returned to our mountain home, and "The Long Walk" is again hanging in my bedroom, the first thing I see when I wake up.

Twenty years later, without any hesitation, Laura Loe generously gave me permission to use to use "The Long Walk" on the cover of this book. Thank you. See more of her art at www.lauraloe.com

ABOUT THE AUTHOR

Nancy Klein Maguire, PhD, came to the Folger Shakespeare Library in 1981 as a dissertation student and never left. She had found her home at the preeminent research library on Shakespeare and early modern history. In 1983, she worked as a research intern, and in 1985, she became a Folger Scholar-In-Residence. During four decades of Folger research, Maguire published two books on seventeenth century theater and multiple articles. Later, she became interested in the relationship between England and France and spent several years studying the role of Charles II's favorite French mistress as a power player in both the French and English courts.

Maguire wrote a major article on the Anglo-French connection in 1993, and, while participating in conferences and seminars, she initiated an international conference on "Europe and Whitehall." In the mid-1990s, she took an unusual sabbatical. She founded and managed a land trust dedicated to saving

North Carolina's Cape Fear from development; she believed humans needed solitude. Through her efforts, the Cape is a dedicated nature preserve.

Since the 2006 publication of her book *An Infinity of Little Hours: Five Young Men and Their Trial of Faith in the Western World's Most Austere Monastic Order*, Maguire's work has been focused on the spirituality of death, dying, and mourning. Drawing from the twenty-six month experience she shared with her late husband, David, she has just published her latest work: *The Monk's Widow: a memoir of resilient love and intimate death.*

DISCUSSION QUESTIONS FOR BOOK GROUP

- What options did David have after we decided to not seek further medical treatment?
- What options did I have?
- Would you want the extra time that we had? Why?
- Would you have continued seeking experimental medical treatment? Why?
- Do you approve of medically assisted death?
- Should we have divorced? When?
- How aware have you been of people dying alone during covid 19? How have you reacted to these couples?
- Would David like this book? What would he have changed in the book?
- Would he have wanted you to write it?
- Did David find his God?
- What did you learn about yourself while you were reading this book?

DISCUSSION QUESTIONS FOR BOOK GROUP

Questions to Ask the Author

- Why do you write? When did you start writing? Why did you write this book?
- In your text you refer to "David's God," do you have a God?
- How do you feel about the people you counted on that were not there when you needed them?
- Why didn't you have a grief therapist?
- How did you feel about people dying alone during covid 19?
- How is being The Monk's Widow different from being any other widow?
- What do you regret?
- Were some chapters harder to write than others? Which ones were the hardest?
- How did you remember what happened?
- How did your life as a scholar influence this book?

Go to https://www.nancykleinmaguire.com/the-monks-widow.html#monks_questions